Preview of
File Folder Family Home Evenings

12 New Testament Themes to Make Learning Fun!

Is preparing family home evening too often a mad dash to throw a lesson together? Then you need *File Folder Family Home Evenings* where everything, except your family can be conveniently stored in a simple file folder.

This unique book combines important gospel lessons with fun, memorable lessons, activities, games, and refreshments to help children learn about Jesus and his ministry. For example, as children learn about Christ's twelve apostles, they can fish for prizes that show ways they can be a missionary. In learning about the Beatitudes, they have a memorable experience playing the *Bee-attitude Blockbuster Quiz Game*. The *Tell Me the Stories of Jesus Match Game* (shown below) will help children learn about the parables in a new and fun way.

The folder size show-and-tell presentations and activities allow you to create a family home evening or CLASS PRESENTATIONS in minutes, then file the activities away to use again and again. Simply photocopy the patterns, color, cut them out, and place them in a file folder.

With *File Folder Family Home Evenings*, you'll have everything you need to quickly prepare creative and effective family nights. Your children will love them, too. In fact, with lessons so fun and easy to put together, they may never let you teach again! Plus, this book is available in CD-ROM.

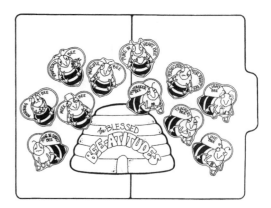

This Book Contains the Following Themes for Your Enjoyment.

- HEAVENLY TREASURES: Follow the Straight and Narrow Path
- SEEDS OF FAITH: My Testimony is Growing
- ANGEL TELLS OF TWO BIRTHS: John and Jesus
- LET'S CELEBRATE the Birth of Jesus
- CREATING ME: I'm Trying to Be Like Jesus
- FISHERS OF MEN: Jesus Choose 12 Apostles
- BLESSED BEATITUDES:
  Jesus Gave the Sermon on the Mount
- THE GIFTS HE GAVE:
  Tell Me the Stories of Jesus
- SERVICE WITH A SMILE:
  Jesus Performed Miracles
- CHOOSE THE RIGHT:
  Jesus Is Our Light
- CAPTAIN OF OUR SHIP:
  Jesus Is Our Life Savior
- IN HIS STEPS:
  Spotlighting the Life of Jesus

W9-BOB-374

Introduction

Primary Partners New Testament, Ages 8-11

46 Lesson Match Activities for the Primary 7 Manual*

Primary teachers and parents, you'll enjoy using the *Primary Partners* activities to supplement your Primary lessons, enhance family home evenings, and help children learn gospel principles in fun, creative ways. Children love these easy, fun-to-create visuals. Patterns for each project are actual size, ready to Copy-n-Create in minutes to make learning fun.

To Make it Easier to Color or Copy Images you will also find this book on CD-ROM to print images instantly from your home computer in full color or black and white. Just ask for the *Primary Partners New Testament* CD-ROM (shown right).

How to Use This Book

• **Use the 1–46 Table of Contents** to match your lessons.

• **Use the A–Z Contents** to find pictures and gospel subjects.

• **Lesson Activities** correlate with specific parts of the lesson. For example, Lesson 1 SCRIPTURES: New Testament Bookmark activity (page 1–2)

correlates with page 3 in the Primary 7 New Testament Manual* (notice the box next to each activity, e.g., shown right).

> Activity Corresponds with the Enrichment Activity #1 (page 3) in the *Primary 7 New Testament Manual.*

• **Gospel Activity Notebook:** Provide each child with a binder or folder to store activities. Encourage children to display activities in their room before placing them in their notebook. Place this "I'm Trying to Be Like Jesus" cover page in the front of their notebook. This cover page (shown left, follows this Introduction). They can place their picture next to Jesus. Children can fill in their personal goals and information.

---

*Primary 7 Manual Is Published by the Church of Jesus Christ of Latter-day Saints, Salt Lake City, Utah.

Primary Partners®
New Testament—Ages 8-11

**Fun Activities that Correlate with the *Primary 7* Manual
with Matching Thought Treats and Scripture Challenge Cards**

Use for Primary Lessons,
Family Home Evening,
and Daily Devotionals to Reinforce
Gospel Topics

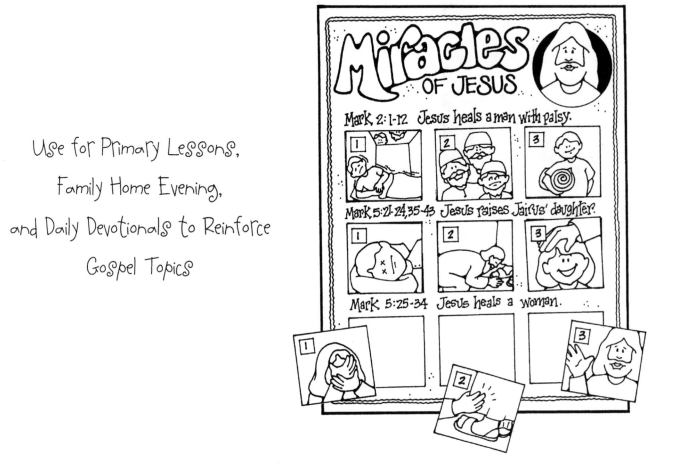

You'll Find: A–Z Topics to Match Primary Lessons 1–46

Apostles   Atonement   Baptism   Commandments   Faith
Fellowship   Forgiveness   Godhead   Good Shepherd
Gratitude   Holy Ghost   Honesty   Jesus Christ
John the Baptist   Love and Compassion   Love Others
Miracles   Mission   Missionary   Parables   Prayer
Priesthood   Repentance   Respect   Resurrection
Sabbath Day   Sacrament   Scriptures   Second Coming
Sermon on the Mount   Service   Service
Speech   Spiritual Gifts   Talents   Temptation
Testimony   Tithes and Offerings

Introducing the Author and Illustrator, Creators of the Following Series of Books and CD-ROMS:

Primary Partners® manual match activities, sharing time, singing fun, and Achievement Days, *Young Women Fun-tastic! Activities for Manuals 1-3 and Personal Progress Motivators, Gospel Fun Activities, Super Singing Activities, Super Little Singers, File Folder Family Home Evenings*, and *Home-spun Fun Family Home Evenings*

Mary Ross, Author

Mary Ross is an energetic mother, and has been a Primary teacher, and Achievement Days leader. She loves to help children and young women have a good time while learning. She has studied acting, modeling, and voice. Her varied interests include writing, creating activities and children's parties, and cooking. Mary and her husband, Paul, live with their daughter, Jennifer, in Sandy, Utah.

Jennette Guymon-King, Illustrator

Jennette Guymon-King has studied graphic arts and illustration at Utah Valley College and the University of Utah. She served a mission to Japan. Jennette enjoys sports, reading, cooking, art, gardening, and freelance illustrating. Jennette and her husband Clayton, live in Riverton, Utah. They are the proud parents of their daughter Kayla Mae, and sons Levi and Carson.

Covenant Communications, Inc.
American Fork, Utah

Printed in Canada
First Printing: July 1998

Primary Partners® *New Testament, Ages 8-11*
ISBN 1-59156-137-X

ACKNOWLEDGEMENTS: Thanks to Inspire Graphics (www.inspiregraphics.com) for the use of Lettering Delights computer font "Twiggy" used in the text.

- **Prepare Treats:** Purchase ingredients to make *Thought Treats*. Treats may not be appropriate for class or sharing time.

- **Copy Patterns Several Weeks Ahead.** You'll save time and avoid last-minute preparations (sample shown right).

- **Shop Ahead for Simple Supplies.** Activities require a few basic items: Copies of patterns, scissors, light/pastel markers or crayons, tape, glue, zip-close plastic bags, paper punch, yarn or ribbon, metal brads (paper fasteners), and pencils.

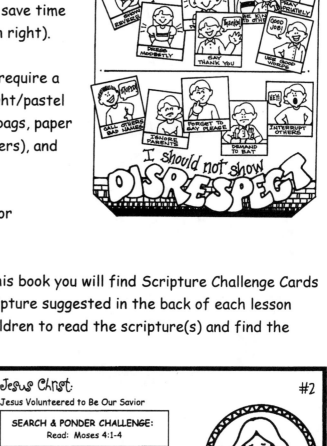

- **Organize Activities** 1–46 for Primary lessons or A-Z for family home evening and Sharing Time.

- **Scripture Challenge Cards:** In the back of this book you will find Scripture Challenge Cards (sample shown right) that correlate with the scripture suggested in the back of each lesson manual (see *Note* below). The cards challenge children to read the scripture(s) and find the missing words (searching the scriptures). They can then place the sticker over the small matching image on the card indicating that their testimony grows as they read the scriptures.

Ways to Use Cards:

1. Have them look up the cards in class before the lesson, keeping the cards in the classroom until the end of the year; placing the sticker on the card after they read them.

2. Give them a card each week with the sticker to take home and add to their book.

3. Make up the complete book and ask them to keep the books at home, reminding them to do the Scripture Challenge each week.

To Make: Punch holes in book and attach with a ribbon or string or cut the cards out and place in a plastic bag. Place label in front of cards.

> *Note:* In the back of each lesson you will find the *Suggested Home Reading*, e.g., for lesson 2: "Suggest that the children study Moses 4:1-4 (shown above) at home as a review of this lesson." You will find these scriptures on each of the 1–46 SCRIPTURE CHALLENGE CARDS.

My Gospel Activity Notebook

I'm Trying to Be Like Jesus

Picture of Me at Age _____

I Will Search, Ponder, and Pray,
and Try to Be More Like Jesus Each Day.
I Will Read the Scriptures Daily.

My Gospel in Action Goals:

ARTICLES OF FAITH Memorization Checklist:

1 ☐ 2 ☐ 3 ☐ 4 ☐ 5 ☐ 6 ☐ 7 ☐ 8 ☐ 9 ☐ 10 ☐ 11 ☐ 12 ☐ 13 ☐

Table of Contents
Primary Partners – New Testament, Ages 8-11

* Primary 7 Manual Is Published by the Church of Jesus Christ of Latter-day Saints, Salt Lake City, Utah.

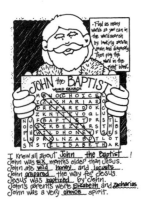

40-MISSIONARY: Teach Gospel (Mission Statement Decode), 79, 81

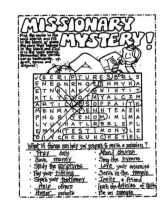

44-MISSIONARY: Prepare Now (Missionary Mystery! Search), 87–88

17-PARABLES: I Will Live Like Jesus (Parable Puzzle), 28–30

11-PRAYER: Pray to Keep Heaven in Sight (Prayer Chart), 17–18

15-PRIESTHOOD: Heavenly Keys (Priesthood Keys Crossword), 24–25

30-REPENTANCE: Overcoming Sin and Death (Repentance Puzzle), 56, 58

8-RESPECT: Show Respect (Choices with Glue–on Stickers), 10, 12–13

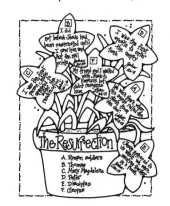

33-RESURRECTION: Jesus & a New Beginning (Flower Pot Quiz), 65, 68

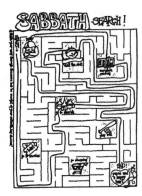

14-SABBATH DAY: Good Activities ("Sabbath Search" Maze), 20, 23

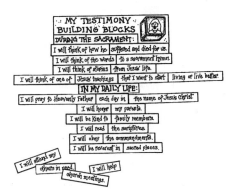

29-SACRAMENT: Think of Jesus (Testimony Building Blocks), 56–57

1-SCRIPTURES: I Will Follow Jesus (New Testament Bookmark), 1–2

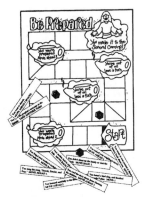

25-SECOND COMING: To See Jesus (Be Prepared Board Game), 47–49

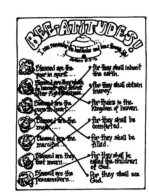

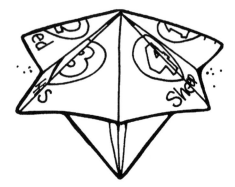

Lesson 1	Scriptures: I Will Read the Scriptures to Learn of Jesus
	(New Testament Bookmark)

YOU'LL NEED: *Copy of *New Testament Bookmark* (page 2) and *Scripture Challenge Card 1* (page 93) on cardstock paper for each child; scissors, markers, yarn or ribbon, and Rubbermaid Contact peel-and-apply paper (for laminating in class) or laminate bookmarks ahead of time.

ACTIVITIES: • *New Testament Bookmark:* Use this bookmark to help children memorize the books of the New Testament in order. Challenge them to say, "I will be valiant and follow Jesus," each time they read the scriptures. (1) *Color and cut out bookmark. (2) Laminate bookmarks in class using the Contact peel-and-apply paper. (3) Paper punch a hole at the top and tie on several strands of yarn or ribbon.
• *Scripture Challenge:* See details on page 93 (card on page 94).

Review the Enrichment Activity 1 (page 3) in the *Primary 7 New Testament Manual.*

THOUGHT TREAT (when appropriate): Seeds of Faith Watermelon Cookies. Make round sugar cookies, cut in half, frost with red frosting and green on the edge (rind), and top with miniature chocolate chips. *Read Matthew 17:20* as you munch on these watermelon-shaped cookies. Tell children that the scriptures will help them plant seeds of faith each day to increase their faith in Jesus Christ and be valiant.

Lesson 2	Jesus Christ: Jesus Volunteered to Be Our Savior
	(John 15:13 Bite-size Memorize Poster)

YOU'LL NEED: *Copy of *Bite-size Memorize Poster* (page 3) and *Scripture Challenge Card 2* (page 93) on cardstock for each child; scissors and markers.

ACTIVITIES: • *Bite-size Memorize:*
*Color and cut out poster for each child. Use this poster to help children memorize John 15:13. Tell children that in the premortal life Jesus volunteered to be our Savior. Learning this scripture will help them feel a greater love for Jesus Christ.
• *Scripture Challenge:* See details on page 93 (card on page 94).

Review the Enrichment Activity 3 (page 8) in the *Primary 7 New Testament Manual.*

THOUGHT TREAT (when appropriate): Life Preserver-Shaped Treats. Share with children a doughnut or Lifesavers candy and tell them that Jesus is our Life Savior.

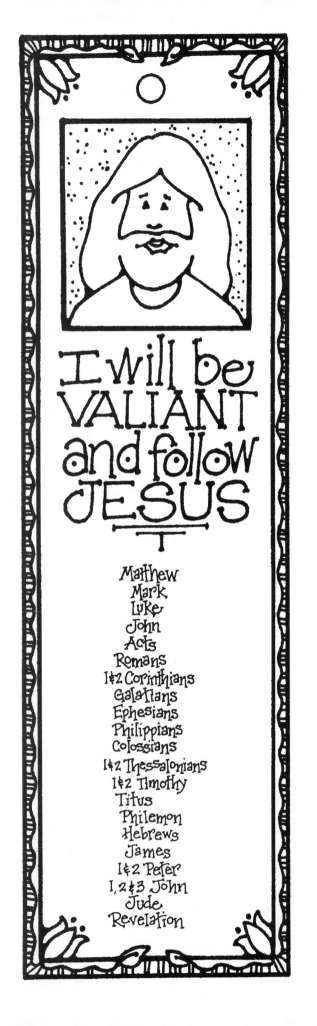
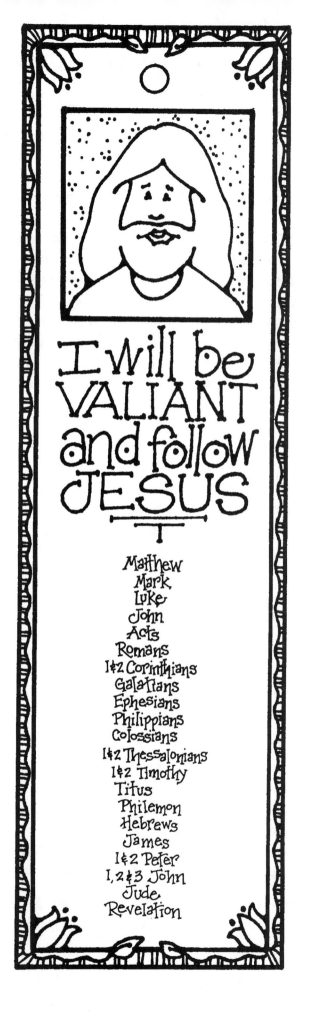

Lesson 3 — John the Baptist: John Prepared the Way for Jesus

(John the Baptist Word Search)

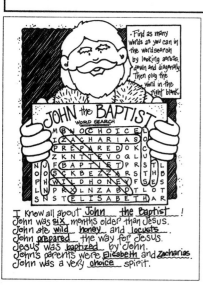

I know all about John the Baptist! John was six months older than Jesus. John ate wild honey and locusts. John prepared the way for Jesus. Jesus was baptized by John. John's parents were Elisabeth and Zacharias. John was a very choice spirit.

YOU'LL NEED: *Copy of *John the Baptist Word Search* (page 5) and *Scripture Challenge Card 3* (page 94) on cardstock paper for each child; scissors and crayons. *Option:* Copy or write out the scripture references for treat below.

ACTIVITIES: • *Word Search:* John the Baptist was chosen to prepare the way for Jesus Christ. Help children learn about John the Baptist. Follow instructions on word search. *Answers:* "I know all about <u>John the Baptist</u>! John was <u>six</u> months older than Jesus. John ate <u>wild honey</u> and <u>locusts</u>. John <u>prepared</u> the way for Jesus. Jesus was <u>baptized</u> by John. John's parents were <u>Zacharias</u> and <u>Elisabeth</u>. John was a very <u>choice</u> spirit."
• *Scripture Challenge:* See details on page 93 (card on page 94).

Review the Enrichment Activity 1 (page 10) in the *Primary 7 New Testament Manual.*

THOUGHT TREAT (when appropriate): Baptism Biscuits or Muffins. Help children learn about John the Baptist and his purpose by stuffing scriptures inside a treat for children to find and read. Purchase or make biscuits or muffins. Write the following scripture references on strips of paper, roll up and place inside biscuit or muffin (pierce with a knife and slide scripture in hole). Wrap scripture references in aluminum foil if baking them inside biscuits or muffins. As children eat their Baptism Biscuits or Muffins, they can find the scripture reference. Have one child with clean hands look up the reference and read it aloud. Provide wet wipes. *Scripture References:* Matthew 3:16 Mark 1:4 John 3:5 Acts 2:38 2 Nephi 31:17 3 Nephi 11:34 Doctrine and Covenants 68:8

Lesson 4 — Jesus Christ: Jesus Is Heavenly Father's Son

("Jesus Is Our Light" Sun-catcher)

He is Heavenly Father's only begotten Son.

YOU'LL NEED: *Copy of *Jesus Is Our Light Sun-catcher* (page 6) and *Scripture Challenge Card 4* (page 94) on cardstock paper for each child; scissors, straight pins or tacks, and markers.

ACTIVITIES: • *Sun-catcher:* Create a sun-catcher poster children can place in their window to let the light shine through, showing that "Jesus Is Our Light." Tell children that Jesus is Heavenly Father's Only Begotten Son, sent to earth to become our light, to show us the way back to our heavenly home. By learning about Jesus and His teachings, we can return to our Heavenly Father someday. Talk about our premortal life and how Jesus was chosen to be the Savior of all mankind. *To Create Sun-catcher:* (1) *Color and cut out sun-catcher. (2) Punch holes in the picture with a pin or tack to define the image of Jesus. (3) Hold picture up to the sun to reflect the light of Jesus. Ask children to tell you something they know about Jesus that is important to them. (4) Tell children they can "catch" the spirit of the Savior's love as they see the sun come through this sun-catcher. They can also catch the spirit of the Savior's love as they read about him in the scriptures. • *Scripture Challenge:* See details on page 93 (card on page 94).

Review the Enrichment Activity 2 (page 13) in the *Primary 7 New Testament Manual.*

THOUGHT TREAT (when appropriate): Sunshine Cookies. Frost round sugar cookies with yellow frosting and add a candy face.

JOHN the BAPTIST
WORD SEARCH

• Find as many words as you can in the wordsearch by looking across, down and diagonally. Then plug the word in the right blank.

```
M B N O C H O I C E L
I Z A C H A R I A S O
P R E P A R E D O K C
Z K N T T E V O Q L U
N J F B A P T I S T P R S T L
O O S C K B E Z Z A R S T H B
P H W I L D H O N E Y F S E S
L N P R X L N Z A B D T L O T
S N S T E L I S A B E T H A R
```

I Know all about _____!
John was ____ months older than Jesus.
John ate _____ and _____.
John _____ the way for Jesus.
Jesus was _____ by John.
John's parents were _____ and _____.
John was a very _____ spirit.

Jesus is our LIGHT

He is Heavenly Father's only begotten Son.

Lesson 5   **Jesus' Childhood:** I Can Become like Jesus

(Luke 2:52 Bite-size Memorize Sticker Poster)

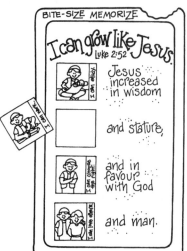

YOU'LL NEED: *Copy of *Bite-size Memorize Sticker Poster* and glue-on *Stickers* (8) and *Scripture Challenge Card 5* (page 95) on cardstock paper for each child; scissors, glue, and markers.

ACTIVITIES: · *Bite-size Memorize Sticker Poster:* Help children glue matching stickers on poster as they memorize Luke 2:52. Talk about ways they can become like Jesus as they increase mentally ("wisdom"), physically ("stature"), spiritually ("favour with God"), and socially ("favour with man").

> Review the Enrichment Activity 6 (page 17) in the *Primary 7 New Testament Manual.*

· *Scripture Challenge:* See details on page 93 (card on page 95).

THOUGHT TREAT (when appropriate): Balanced Life Balloon Cupcakes. Frost a cupcake for each child and top with four gumdrops or jelly beans. Frost balloon string tails. Tell children they can balance their life as Jesus did in the four balanced life areas.

Lesson 6   **Baptism:** I Will Keep My Baptismal Covenants

(Heaven's Gate to Strait and Narrow Path)

YOU'LL NEED: *Copy of *Heaven's Gate* (page 9) and *Scripture Challenge Card 6* (page 95) on cardstock paper, and a paper fastener (metal brad) for each child; scissors, and markers.

ACTIVITIES: · *Heaven's Gate:* Remind children that they are heaven sent and heaven bound. We came from heaven and if we are to return we must enter the gate of "repentance and baptism by water," receiving the Holy Ghost (read 2 Nephi 31:17). If we follow the

> Review the Enrichment Activity 4 (page 20) in the *Primary 7 New Testament Manual.*

strait and narrow path, relying on Jesus Christ to guide us (2 Nephi 31:18-19), and stay on this path and endure to the end, we will return to Heavenly Father, having eternal life. (Help children memorize 2 Nephi 31:20). *To Create the Gate:* (1) *Color and cut out the baptism gate and the strait and narrow path leading to heaven. (2) Glue baptism gate on the right side of the path where indicated, and fold back gate to swing open. (3) *Optional:* Insert metal brad. Pierce a hole at the top left of the gate post with a metal brad. Insert brad with the round part of the brad on the back of the post and the two prongs in the front. Bend prongs and turn prongs toward the gate to lock the gate, or turn away from the gate to open the gate. · *Scripture Challenge:* See details on page 93 (card on page 95).

THOUGHT TREAT (when appropriate): Graham Cracker Gate. Frost two half size graham crackers on top of each other. Talk about the words on the gate (shown above).

BAPTISM

the gate to the strait and narrow path.

---

glue gate here

I WANT TO STAY ON THE STRAIT AND NARROW PATH!

As a member I will:

- Help and love others.
- Stand as a witness of Heavenly Father and Jesus at all times wherever I go!
- Keep Heavenly Father's commandments.

I'm heaven sent and heaven bound.

Lesson 7   Temptation: I Will Follow Jesus and Resist Temptation

("I Have a Strong Spirit! I Can Say No!" Poster)

YOU'LL NEED: *Copy of *I Have a Strong Spirit! Poster* (page 11) and *Scripture Challenge Card 7* (page 96) on cardstock paper for each child; scissors, and markers.

ACTIVITIES: · *I Have a Strong Spirit Poster:* *Color poster and read Corinthians 10:13. Help children to make a strong decision to say "NO" to temptation with this "I Have a Strong Spirit!" poster. Ask children to do the following (found on poster): ➤*Decide* to choose the right by thinking ahead what you will do when temptation comes. ➤*Pray* to avoid temptation, knowing that Heavenly Father will help you. ➤*Listen* to the Holy Ghost as the Spirit tells you what is right and wrong. ➤*Know* that Heavenly Father loves you and will help you.
· *Scripture Challenge:* See details on page 93 (card on page 96).

> Review the Enrichment Activity 5 (page 23) in the *Primary 7 New Testament Manual.*

THOUGHT TREAT (when appropriate): Say "Yes!" Healthy Snacks. Enjoy munching on healthy snacks with the children. Tell them that these are good foods Heavenly Father has given us to choose from. Just as there are good and bad foods, there are good and bad choices each day. Let's turn our thoughts to good things and we will be happy.

Lesson 8   Respect: I Will Show Heavenly Father and Jesus Respect

(Respectful Choices Poster)

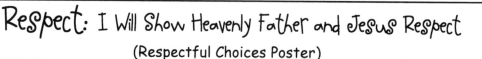

YOU'LL NEED: *Copy of *I Can Show Respect Poster* and glue on stickers (pages 12-13) and *Scripture Challenge Card 8* (page 96) on cardstock paper for each child; scissors, glue, and markers.

ACTIVITIES: · *I Can Show Respect Poster*: *Color and cut out choices (glue-on stickers). Encourage children to make good choices ahead of time by matching the glue-on sticker pictures with the RESPECT and DISRESPECT categories on the chart. Discuss why respectful choices please Heavenly Father and Jesus.
· *Scripture Challenge:* See details on page 93 (card on page 96).

> Review the Attention Activity (page 25) in the *Primary 7 New Testament Manual.*

THOUGHT TREAT (when appropriate): CTR Cookies. Frost the letters "CTR" on a cookie to remind children that as they choose the right each day, they are showing respect and love from Heavenly Father and Jesus.

Lesson 9   Apostles: The Apostles Were Special Witnesses of Jesus
(Apostle Match Game)

YOU'LL NEED: *Copy two sets of *Apostle Match Game* cards (page 15) *and Scripture Challenge Card 9* (page 97) for each child; scissors, and markers.

ACTIVITIES: • *Apostle Match Game:* Play the *Apostles Match Game* to learn about the 12 Apostles that Jesus chose to lead His church. Talk about the Apostles chosen. Explain that the Apostles were teachers, examples, and special witnesses of Jesus Christ. They followed Jesus and taught others about the plan of salvation. They taught what He taught, they wrote about Him in the scriptures.

> Review the Enrichment Activity 2 (page 31) in the *Primary 7 New Testament Manual.*

They tried to live as He did. *To Make Game:* *Color and cut out two sets of apostle cards. *To Play The Match Game:* (1) Divide class into two teams. (2) Lay cards facedown. (3) Teams take turns drawing two cards to make a match. When a match is made, say the two Apostles' names aloud. (4) When all cards are matched, the team with the most matches wins. (5) If the cards "Special Witness of Jesus" or "Teacher/Example" are matched, take another turn.
• *Scripture Challenge:* See details on page 93 (card on page 97).

THOUGHT TREAT (when appropriate): Example Feet Cookies. Shape fudge or cookie dough into foot shapes and add candies (baking cookies). Feet remind us to follow and walk in the footsteps of Jesus like His Apostles did.

Lesson 10   Sermon on the Mount: Jesus Taught Us How to Return to Heaven
("Bee"-atitude Cross Match)

YOU'LL NEED: *Copy of *"Bee"-atitude Cross Match* (page 16) and *Scripture Challenge Card 10* (page 97) for each child; scissors, pencils, and markers.

ACTIVITIES: • *"Bee"-atitude Cross Match:* Tell children that Jesus taught the Beatitudes in His Sermon on the Mount, showing us how we can return to heaven. Help children learn the beatitudes (Matthew 5:3–12) and then match the beatitude with the bee. Compare the New Testament references

> Review the Enrichment Activity 7 (page 35) in the *Primary 7 New Testament Manual.*

with the Book of Mormon and write in the translation. See *References* below. Example: *"Blessed are the poor in spirit"* (*"who come unto me"* was left out in the Bible but was given in 3 Nephi 12:3). Remind children of the 8th Article of Faith: *"We believe the Bible to be the word of God as far as it is translated correctly; we also believe the Book of Mormon to be the word of God."* Explain that Jesus gave the Beatitudes while He was living on the earth in the New Testament times. After His death and resurrection, he visited the Nephites on the American continent and gave them the Beatitudes (3 Nephi). *References:* ❤ Matthew 5:3 (missing a part found in 3 Nephi 12:3, *"who come unto me"*) ❤ Matthew 5:6 (missing a part found in 3 Nephi 12:6, *"filled with the Holy Ghost"*) ❤ See the cross references below 3 Nephi 2:10 (Matthew 5:10 and D&C 122:5–9 telling that Joseph Smith was persecuted for righteousness' sake) ❤ Matthew 5:48 and 3 Nephi 12:48 (become *"perfect"* is to become like Heavenly Father and Jesus). • *Scripture Challenge:* See details on p. 93 (card on p. 94).

THOUGHT TREAT (when appropriate): Honey Taffy to remind us of the "bee"-atitudes

BEE-ATITUDES!

I can remember the beatitudes and buzz through life!

Matthew 5:3-12

Blessed are the poor in spirit.... ∘ for they shall inherit the earth.

Blessed are they which do hunger and thirst after righteousness... ∘ for they shall obtain mercy.

Blessed are the pure in heart.... ∘ for theirs is the Kingdom of heaven.

Blessed are the meek.... ∘ for they shall be comforted.

Blessed are the merciful... ∘ for they shall be filled.

Blessed are they that mourn.... ∘ for they shall be called the children of God.

Blessed are the peacemakers... ∘ for they shall see God.

Lesson 11 Prayer: I Will Pray Morning and Night to Keep Heaven in Sight
(Prayer Chart)

YOU'LL NEED: *Copy of *Prayer Chart* (page 18) and *Scripture Challenge Card 11* (page 98) for each child; scissors and markers.

ACTIVITIES: • *Prayer Chart:* (1) Encourage children to *color and mark this daily prayer chart which reminds them to pray morning and night to keep heaven in sight. When they have morning prayer they can color the top portion of the number. When they have evening prayer they can color the bottom portion of the number.

> Review Enrichment Activities 2 and 3 (page 39) in the *Primary 7 New Testament Manual.*

(2) Share special experiences when prayers were answered.
(3) Remind children of the special words we use to refer to God in our prayers that show respect and love for him: Talk about using special prayer words referring to God: *Thee, Thou, Thy*, and *Thine*. • *Scripture Challenge:* See details on page 93 (card on page 98).

THOUGHT TREAT (when appropriate): Smile Face Fudge. Shape fudge into balls, press down, and carve a smile with the round edge of a spoon and the eyes with the pointed end. Quick Fudge Recipe: Melt an 11-ounce package of milk chocolate chips, 7 ounces sweetened condensed milk, and 1 tsp. vanilla in microwave (about 2-6 minutes). While hot, drop by teaspoonsful onto waxed paper. Mold into balls, then press balls to 1/4".

Lesson 12 Commandments: The Gospel of Jesus Christ Is My Firm Foundation
("Build upon My Rock" Rock and Body Puzzle)

YOU'LL NEED: *Copy of *Rock and Body Puzzle* (page 19) and *Scripture Challenge Card 12* (page 98) on colored cardstock paper for each child; scissors, and markers. *Option 1:* An extra 8 ½" x 11" sheet of contrasting colored cardstock paper (if you are glue-mounting puzzle on paper), *Option 2:* A zip-close plastic sandwich bag (if you are storing puzzle pieces in a bag).

ACTIVITIES: • *Rock and Body Puzzle:* Create a rock and body puzzle to show children ways they can obey the commandments, showing that the gospel of Jesus Christ is our rock. Read, *"Build upon my rock, which is my gospel"* (D&C 11:24), and tell

> Review Enrichment Activity 3 (page 43) in the *Primary 7 New Testament Manual.*

children that Jesus is the rock. He is our Redeemer, the Son of God. We must build a firm foundation by living the gospel of Jesus Christ, or we will not have the power to overcome the mighty winds and storms of the devil, who would *"drag you down into the gulf of misery and endless woe."* (Read Helaman 5:12.) *To Create Rock Puzzle:* (1) Color and cut out rock and body puzzle, using girl or boy head. (2) Put puzzle pieces together. (3) Glue-mount puzzle on an 8 ½" x 11" piece of colored paper, or store in a plastic bag.
• *Scripture Challenge:* See details on page 93 (card on page 98).

THOUGHT TREAT (when appropriate): Rock and Body Cookies. Make gingerbread cookie dough. Roll and cut out gingerbread boys and girls, and then roll the other half of the dough into 2" rocks (dip cookie top in granulated or powdered sugar before baking) at 350° for 8-10 minutes. Decorate cookies.

Lesson 13 — Love and Compassion: I Can Be Like Jesus
(Compassion Wheel)

YOU'LL NEED: *Copy of *Compassion Wheel* (pages 21-22) and *Scripture Challenge Card 13* (page 99) on cardstock paper, and a paper fastener (metal brad) or button brad for each child; scissors, and markers.

ACTIVITIES: · *Compassion Wheel:* Help children learn how to show love and compassion as Jesus did when he healed the sick. *Make Ahead:* (1) *Color and cut out parts A and B. (2) Attach part A on top of part B with a metal or button brad in the center. To make a button brad, sew two buttons together on opposite sides (threading thread through the same hole in the papers) to attach compassion wheels. *In Class:* Have children draw pictures in the blank circles of things they can do to show love and compassion. Read 1 John 3:18 and help children learn how to show love and compassion as Jesus did when He was kind to the children and healed the sick. · *Scripture Challenge:* See page 93 (card on page 99).

> Review Enrichment Activity 2 (page 46) in *Primary 7 New Testament Manual.*

THOUGHT TREAT (when appropriate): Heart-Shaped Pan-wich. Reduce the amount of water in pancake batter by 1 teaspoon and add ½ teaspoon red food coloring. Make two 4" heart-shaped pancakes for each child. Then spread strawberry or raspberry jam in between two layers. Remind children as they eat, that Jesus loves them and wants them to love and show compassion towards others.

Lesson 14 — Sabbath Day: I Will Choose Righteous Sabbath Activities
("Sabbath Search" Maze)

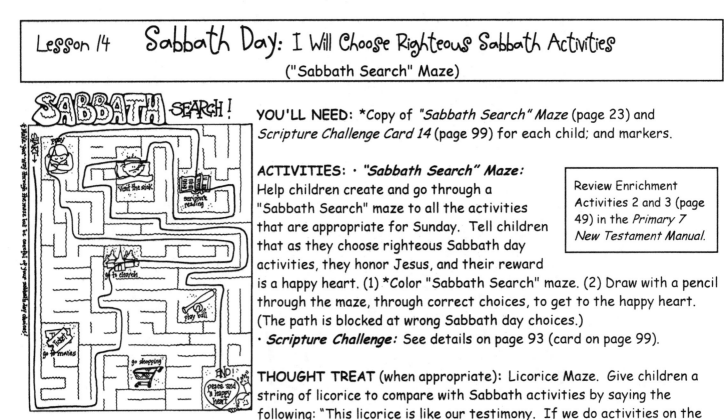

YOU'LL NEED: *Copy of *"Sabbath Search" Maze* (page 23) and *Scripture Challenge Card 14* (page 99) for each child; and markers.

ACTIVITIES: · *"Sabbath Search" Maze:* Help children create and go through a "Sabbath Search" maze to all the activities that are appropriate for Sunday. Tell children that as they choose righteous Sabbath day activities, they honor Jesus, and their reward is a happy heart. (1) *Color "Sabbath Search" maze. (2) Draw with a pencil through the maze, through correct choices, to get to the happy heart. (The path is blocked at wrong Sabbath day choices.) · *Scripture Challenge:* See details on page 93 (card on page 99).

> Review Enrichment Activities 2 and 3 (page 49) in the *Primary 7 New Testament Manual.*

THOUGHT TREAT (when appropriate): Licorice Maze. Give children a string of licorice to compare with Sabbath activities by saying the following: "This licorice is like our testimony. If we do activities on the Sabbath that invite the Spirit, our testimony grows and stretches. (Tie licorice in a knot.) If we do activities on the Sabbath that do not invite the Spirit, our testimony becomes smaller (tied up in knots). Let's name some activities that will help us stretch our testimony of the Sabbath."

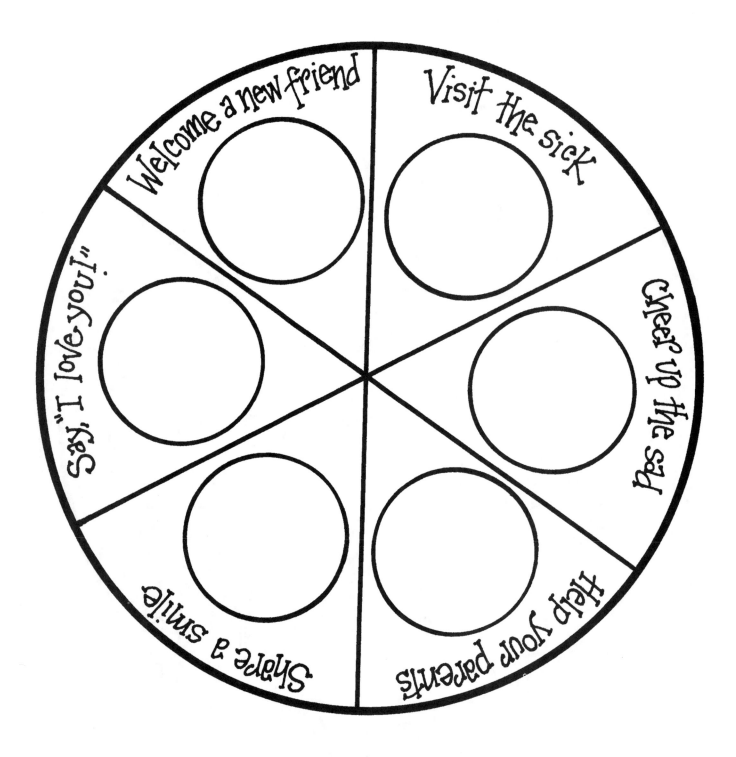

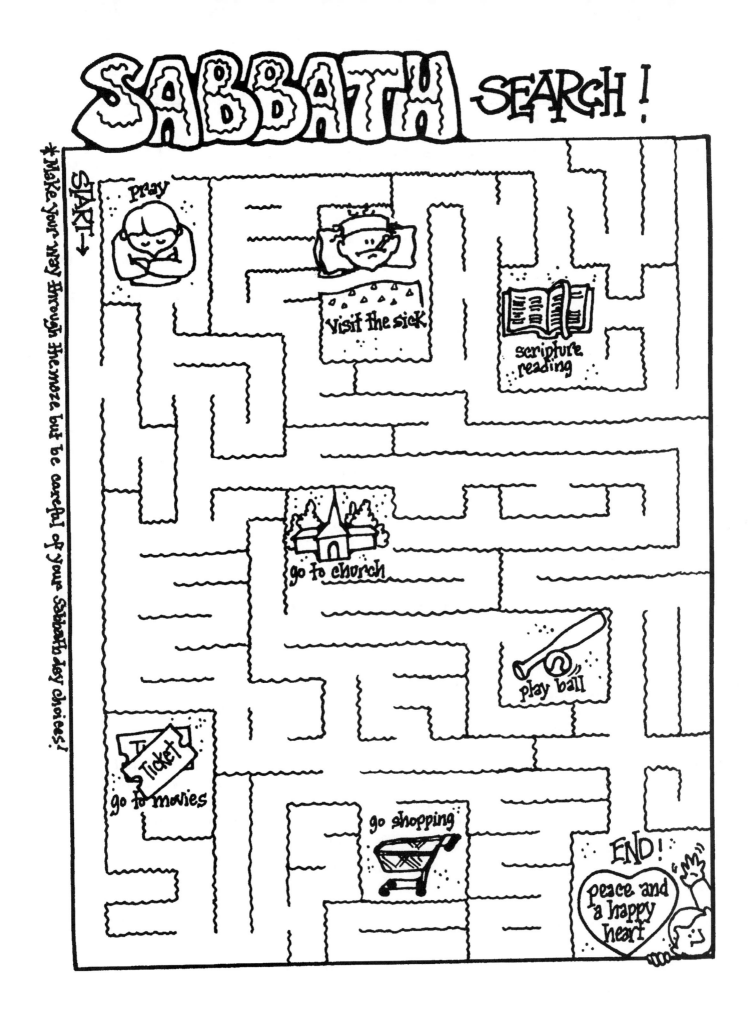

Lesson 15 — Priesthood: Heavenly Keys
(Priesthood Keys Crossword Puzzle)

HEAVENLY KEYS

See what Priesthood Power can do!

*Find the keywords that fit in the crossword with the special clues below!

ACROSS
1. _____ the sick
4. A father's _____
6. God's special power
8. _____ by immersion

DOWN
1. Gift of the _____
2. Ordinances of the _____
3. Bless brand new _____
5. Give babies a _____
7. Bread and water blessed

Review Enrichment Activity 1 (page 52) in the *Primary 7 New Testament Manual.*

YOU'LL NEED: *Copy of *Priesthood Keys Crossword Puzzle* (page 25) and *Scripture Challenge Card 15* (page 100) on cardstock paper for each child; pencils, and markers.

ACTIVITIES: · *Priesthood Keys Crossword Puzzle:* Help children learn about the power of the priesthood by completing this puzzle. The word "PRIESTHOOD" is found in the center and all the other words describe the special powers and blessings that come from the priesthood. *Answers:* Across: 1. heal, 4. blessing, 6. priesthood, 8. baptism. Down: 1. Holy Ghost, 2. temple, 3. babies, 5. name, 7. sacrament.
· *Scripture Challenge:* See details on page 93 (card on p. 100).

THOUGHT TREAT (when appropriate): Priesthood Key Cookies. Create two cookie keys to represent the two priesthoods. Tell children that the two priesthoods given are the Aaronic Priesthood and the Melchizedek Priesthood. Read D&C 13 and 27:12 to tell how these priesthoods were restored. The Melchizedek is the higher Priesthood. The Aaronic is the preparatory priesthood. *To Make Cookies:* Add five drops of yellow food coloring into sugar cookie dough before adding flour. Cut out sugar cookie dough in the shape of two different keys (see keys on crossword puzzle above). Use a straw to make a hole at the top. Bake cookies, cool, and tie two key cookies together with ribbon, yarn, or string.

Lesson 16 — Miracles: Jesus Christ Performed Miracles
(Three Miracles Picture Poster)

Miracles OF JESUS

Mark 2:1-12 Jesus heals a man with palsy.

Mark 5:21-24,35-43 Jesus raises Jairus's daughter.

Mark 5:25-34 Jesus heals a woman.

Review Scripture Accounts 1-3 (pages 54-55) in the *Primary 7 New Testament Manual.*

YOU'LL NEED: *Copy of *Miracles of Jesus Poster* and glue-on stickers (pages 26-27) and *Scripture Challenge Card 16* (page 100) on colored cardstock paper for each child, scissors, glue, and markers.

ACTIVITIES: · *Miracles of Jesus Picture Poster:* Strengthen children's faith in Jesus Christ by reading three miracles Jesus performed. Create a picture poster of these three miracles. (1) *Color and cut out stickers (page 27). (2) Find the three stickers for each miracle and glue them in the right place, numbering the stickers 1, 2, and 3 to determine order of placement on the poster. (3) Encourage children to use poster as a teaching tool to share with their family.
· *Scripture Challenge:* See details on page 93 (card on page 100).

THOUGHT TREAT (when appropriate): Heart-shaped Sandwich. Cut two slices of bread for each child into a heart shape. Fill with cream cheese filling or other sandwich spread. As children enjoy, tell them that Jesus performed miracles because of his love for us. We can now experience the miracles of Jesus through the healing power of the priesthood that was restored to the earth.

HEAVENLY KEYS

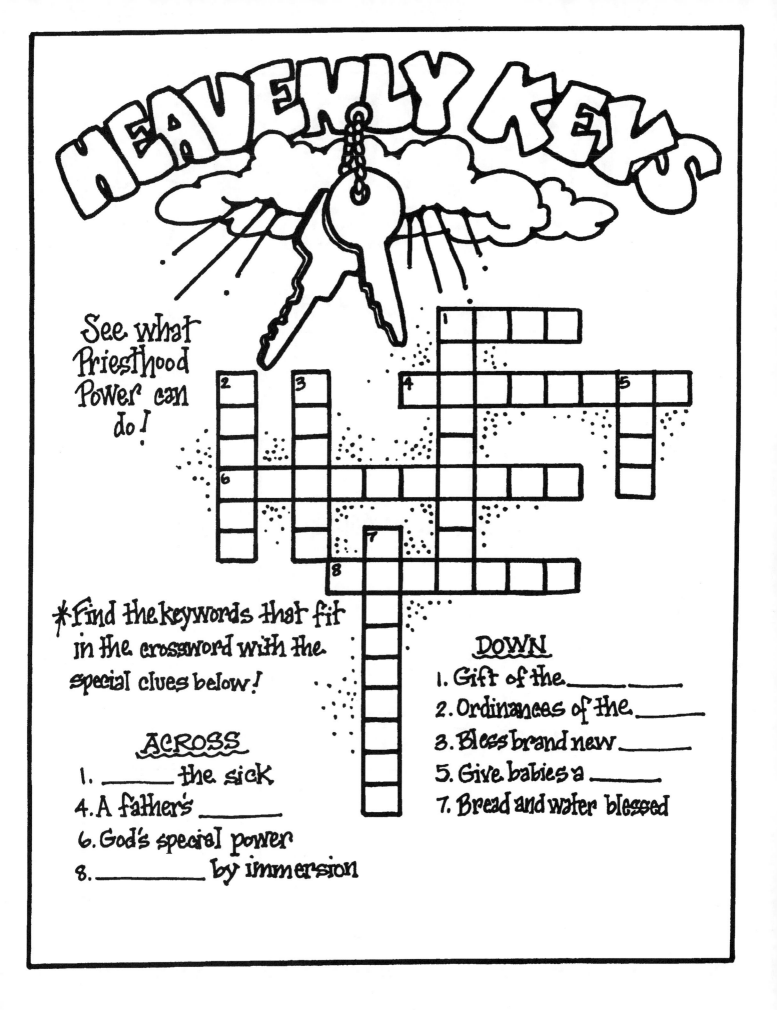

See what Priesthood Power can do!

*Find the keywords that fit in the crossword with the special clues below!

ACROSS

1. _____ the sick
4. A father's _____
6. God's special power
8. _____ by immersion

DOWN

1. Gift of the _____
2. Ordinances of the _____
3. Bless brand new _____
5. Give babies a _____
7. Bread and water blessed

Miracles OF JESUS

Mark 2:1-12 Jesus heals a man with palsy.

Mark 5:21-24,35-43 Jesus raises Jairus's daughter.

Mark 5:25-34 Jesus heals a woman.

Lesson 17 Parables: I Will Live Like Jesus and Keep His Commandments
(Parable Puzzles)

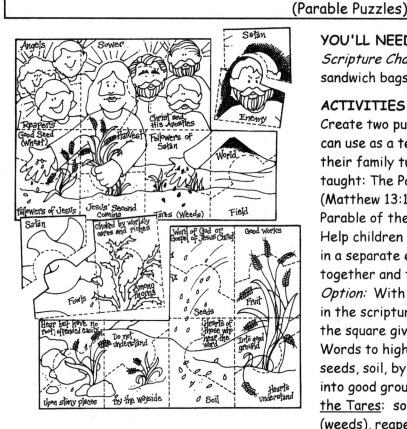

YOU'LL NEED: *Copy two *Parable Puzzles* (pages 29-30), *Scripture Challenge Card 17* (page 101), and two envelopes or sandwich bags for each child; scissors, and markers.

ACTIVITIES: •*Parable Puzzles:* Create two puzzles that children can use as a teaching tool to teach their family two parables Jesus taught: The Parable of the Sower (Matthew 13:1-9, 18-23; Mark 4:14-20; Luke 8:11-15), and the Parable of the Wheat and the Tares (Matthew 13:24-30). Help children color and cut out puzzles and place each puzzle in a separate envelope or plastic bag. Put the puzzles together and then read the parables from the scriptures. *Option:* With a light marker, highlight the key words found in the scriptures and tell children that the other words on the square give the meaning of the words Jesus used. Words to highlight are as follows. Parable of the Sower: seeds, soil, by the wayside, upon stony places, among thorns, into good ground, fowls, and fruit. Parable of the Wheat and the Tares: sower, good seed (wheat), field, enemy, tares (weeds), reapers, and harvest.

> Review Enrichment Activity 1 (page 58) in the *Primary 7 New Testament Manual.*

• *Scripture Challenge:* See details on page 93 (card on page 101).

THOUGHT TREAT (when appropriate): Wheat Treat. Something good made out of wheat, like whole wheat cookies, crackers, or rolls. You might show the children what wheat looks like before it is ground into flour.

Lesson 18 Faith: I Can Overcome Trials with the Help of Jesus
(Blind Puzzle)

YOU'LL NEED: Copy of *Blind Puzzle* (page 31) and *Scripture Challenge Card 18* (page 101) for each child; scissors, and markers.

> Review Enrichment Activity 1 (page 61) in the *Primary 7 New Testament Manual.*

ACTIVITIES: • *Blind Puzzle:* As children put together this puzzle they can think about the faith they have in Jesus Christ and memorize the words: "I can overcome trials and challenges with the help of Jesus Christ." Read: Daniel 3:17-18, 23-25, 28, 1 Nephi 18:16, 20-22, Mosiah 24:13-16, Alma 14:8-11. • *Scripture Challenge:* See details on page 93 (card on page 101).

THOUGHT TREAT (when appropriate): Blindfolded Treats. Place a variety of treats in a bag. Blindfold children or have them close their eyes to reach in a bag and pull out a treat. Have them touch it and smell it and taste it to see if they can tell the others what they have. If they guess it, give them a second treat.

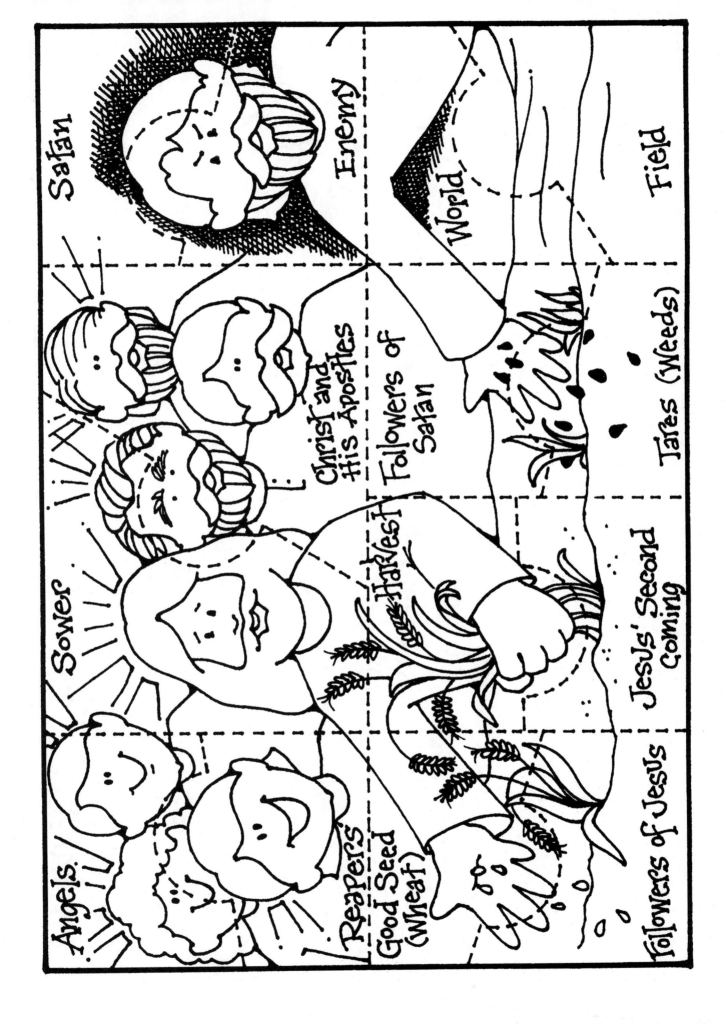

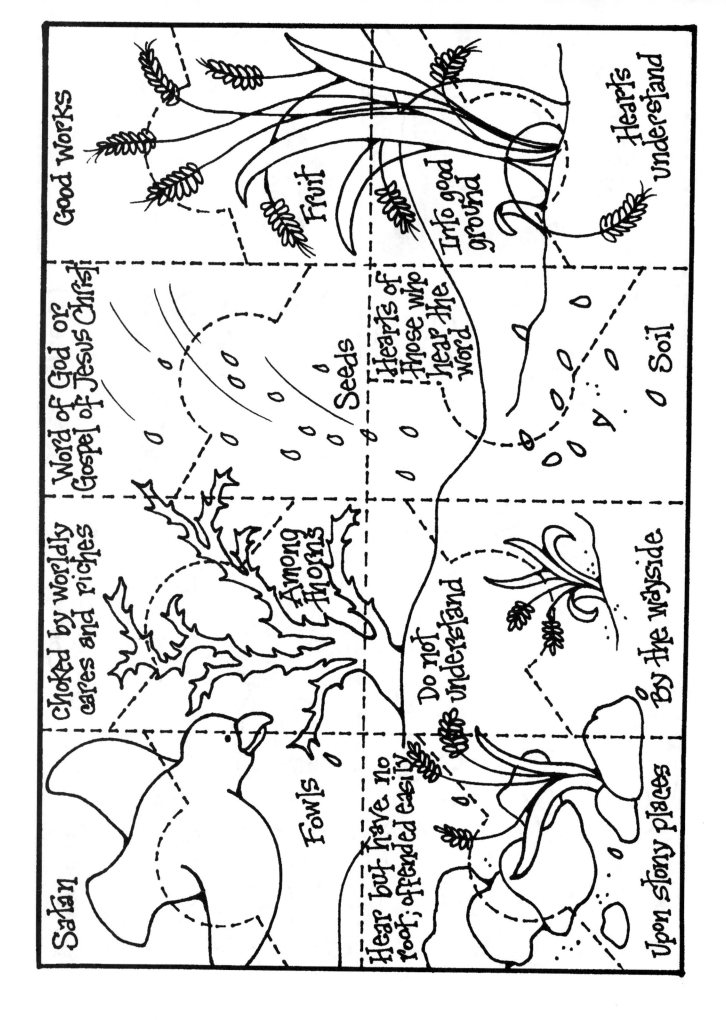

Lesson 19 Fellowship: I Will Help Those Who Are less Active Return
(Find the Lost Pictures - Prodigal Son Poster)

The Lost Sheep · The Lost Coin · The Prodigal Son

Find and circle the lost little sheep, 10 coins, the father and his lost son, and the fatted calf.

YOU'LL NEED:
*Copy of *Prodical Son Poster* (page 33) and Scripture Challenge Card 19 (page 102) on cardstock paper for each child; scissors, and markers.

> Review the Discussions 1 and 2 (pages 63-64) in the *Primary 7 New Testament Manual.*

ACTIVITIES:
• *Prodical Son Poser:* Have children think of those who are less active in the Church and ways they can help them return to activity. Have children think of this as they find the lost sheep, ten coins, the father, the lost son, and the fatted calf (circling or coloring what they find). Read the parables from the scripture references: the Lost Sheep and the Lost Coins (Luke 15:4, 8), and the Prodigal Son (Luke 15:12-32).
• *Scripture Challenge:* See details on page 93 (card on page 101).

THOUGHT TREAT (when appropriate):
Candy or Cookie Coins. Purchase chocolate coins wrapped in gold foil, or make sugar cookies, cutting them out with a bottle lid. Then press a washed coin into cookie before baking. Give each child 10 cookie coins, having children reserve one coin for the one that was lost (in the Parable of the Lost Coin).

The Lost Sheep · The Lost Coin · The Prodigal Son

Find and circle the lost little sheep, 10 coins, the father and his lost son, and the fatted calf.

Lesson 20	Love Others:
	I Will Show Love Like the Good Samaritan
	(Love-Lingo! Bingo)

YOU'LL NEED: *Copy of *Love-Lingo! Bingo* cards and markers (pages 35-39), *Love-Lingo* calling words (shown left), and Scripture Challenge Card 20 (page 103) on colored cardstock paper; scissors, and markers. *Optional:* Make a copy of *Bingo* game for each child.

Review the Enrichment Activity 1 (page 67) in the *Primary 7 New Testament Manual.*

ACTIVITIES: • *Love-Lingo! Bingo:* Help children increase their desire to show love as the Good Samaritan did. Tell the story, and then help them match good deeds on the Love-Lingo! Bingo cards.

To Play:
1. Explain to children that "lingo" means language and give each child a different Love-Lingo! Bingo card and 25 Love-Lingo markers.
2. Place the words (shown left) on slips of paper to draw from a container and read. Children can say, "Love-Lingo! Bingo," if they have marked five in a row, up, down, or diagonally. Have them place a marker in the center to begin.

• *Scripture Challenge:* See details on page 93 (card on page 103).

THOUGHT TREAT (when appropriate): Crackers from the Heart. Decorate crackers with processed cheese, making a heart on each cracker. Tell children that the Good Samaritan fed the poor man who was laying on the road. The charity that the Samaritan showed tells us that he had a good heart.

LOVE-LINGO! BINGO CALLING WORDS:
say please
clean up room
tend baby sister
call a friend
read story to a child
walk quietly in the chapel
visit a sick friend
make a special card
listen
speak kind words
invite a friend to church
welcome a new friend
take turns
invite a friend over
be thankful
say hello
smile
make a treat
help with dishes
be courteous
be friendly
show kindness
say "I love you!"
speak reverently about Jesus
respect others' property
share a happy thought
pray for someone
cheer up the sad
follow the golden rule
keep promises

Love BINGO

Card 2

BINGO

Keep a promise	Be a friend	Clean up room	Be thankful	Share a happy thought
Invite a friend over	Speak reverently about Jesus	Smile	Say please	Welcome a new friend
Call a friend	Take turns	FREE Good Samaritan	Make a special card	Read a story to a child
Tend baby sister	Help with the dishes	Make a treat	Listen politely	Visit a sick friend
Show Kindness	Say hello	Say I love you	Say Kind words	Walk quietly in the chapel

Love BINGO

Card 1

BINGO

Say I love you	Clean up room	Take turns	Listen politely	Say Kind words
Walk quietly in the chapel	Make a treat	Tend baby sister	Smile	Visit a sick friend
Read a story to a child	Show Kindness	FREE Good Samaritan	Call a friend	Speak reverently about Jesus
Be a friend	Help with the dishes	Keep a promise	Say hello	Welcome a new friend
Invite a friend over	Be thankful	Make a special card	Be courteous	Say please

Love LINGO! BINGO

Invite a friend to church	Be a friend	Be thankful	Welcome a new friend	Take turns
Visit a sick friend	Clean up room	Call a friend	Keep a promise	Show kindness
Listen politely	Say please	FREE God Samaritan	Walk quietly in the chapel	Cheer up the sad
Tend baby sister	Invite a friend over	Say hello	Speak reverently about Jesus	Read a story to a child
Say kind words	Help with the dishes	Say I love you	Make a treat	Make a special card

Love LINGO! BINGO

Say I love you	Help with the dishes	Tend baby sister	Be a friend	Invite a friend over
Say kind words	Listen politely	Show kindness	Say hello	Speak reverently about Jesus
Clean up room	Make a treat	FREE God Samaritan	Read a story to a child	Be thankful
Make a special card	Visit a sick friend	Welcome a new friend	Call a friend	Keep a promise
Cheer up the sad	Take turns	Say please	Invite a friend to church	Walk quietly in the chapel

Love LINGO

BINGO

Respect others' property	Welcome a new friend	Read a story to a child	Be thankful	Keep a promise
Walk quietly in the chapel	Make a special card	Clean up room	Be a friend	Say hello
Invite a friend over	Show kindness	FREE Good Samaritan	Make a treat	Listen politely
Tend baby sister	Say kind words	Say I love you	Say please	Speak reverently about Jesus
Visit a sick friend	Help with the dishes	Call a friend	Take turns	Smile

---

Love LINGO

BINGO

Say please	Invite a friend over	Take turns	Make a treat	Help with the dishes
Say kind words	Smile	Speak reverently about Jesus	Listen politely	Show Kindness
Tend baby sister	Visit a sick friend	FREE Good Samaritan	Walk quietly in the chapel	Say hello
Be a friend	Say I love you	Make a special card	Be thankful	Welcome a new friend
Read a story to a child	Keep a promise	Clean up room	Pray for someone	Call a friend

Love LINGO! BINGO

Invite a friend to church	Say hello	Invite a friend over	Call a friend	Say kind words
Read a story to a child	Say please	Show kindness	Help with the dishes	Visit a sick friend
Walk quietly in the chapel	Welcome a new friend	FREE Good Samaritan	Tend baby sister	Make a treat
Keep a promise	Say I love you	Clean up room	Take turns	Cheer up the sad
Speak reverently about Jesus	Be thankful	Be a friend	Make a special card	Listen politely

8

Love LINGO! BINGO

Be a friend	Cheer up the sad	Walk quietly in the chapel	Invite a friend over	Say please
Take turns	Say kind words	Welcome a new friend	Clean up room	Show kindness
Make a special card	Help with the dishes	FREE Good Samaritan	Tend baby sister	Be thankful
Say hello	Read a story to a child	Speak reverently about Jesus	Visit a sick friend	Invite a friend to church
Say I love you	Keep a promise	Call a friend	Listen politely	Make a treat

7

Lesson 21   Gratitude: Jesus Healed Ten Lepers and Only One Thanked Him
(Jesus Thank-you Card)

Jesus healed 10 lepers and only one returned to say **Thank you!** Can you name 10 things you could thank Jesus for?

10. _____

YOU'LL NEED: *Copy of *Jesus Thank-you Card* (page 41) and *Scripture Challenge Card 21* (page 104) on cardstock paper, and a pencil for each child; scissors and markers.

ACTIVITIES: • *Jesus Thank-you Card:* Help children create a personal thank-you card to Heavenly Father and Jesus to remind them of

> Review Enrichment Activities 2 and 4 (page 70) in the *Primary 7 New Testament Manual.*

the many blessings they receive. (1) *Color and cut out thank-you card. (2) Write in #1–10 the things you would thank Jesus for. (3) Take these home and when you say your prayers, remember to mention the things on the list. (4) Fold card to place inside your scriptures and read often.
• *Scripture Challenge:* See details on page 93 (card on page 104).

THOUGHT TREAT (when appropriate): Blessing Berries. Give each child two strawberries. As they eat, ask them to share one or two blessings with the class.

Lesson 22   Forgiveness: I Will Be Merciful and Forgiving
(Scripture Search Wall Hanging)

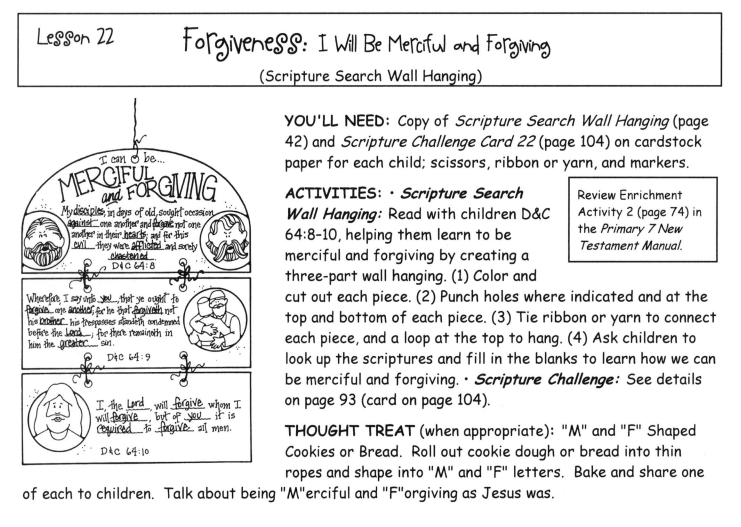

I can be... **MERCIFUL and FORGIVING**

My disciples, in days of old, sought occasion against one another and forgave not one another in their hearts; and for this evil they were afflicted and sorely chastened. D&C 64:8

Wherefore, I say unto you, that ye ought to forgive one another; for he that forgiveth not his brother his trespasses standeth condemned before the Lord; for there remaineth in him the greater sin.
D&C 64:9

I, the Lord, will forgive whom I will forgive, but of you it is required to forgive all men.
D&C 64:10

YOU'LL NEED: Copy of *Scripture Search Wall Hanging* (page 42) and *Scripture Challenge Card 22* (page 104) on cardstock paper for each child; scissors, ribbon or yarn, and markers.

ACTIVITIES: • *Scripture Search Wall Hanging:* Read with children D&C 64:8-10, helping them learn to be merciful and forgiving by creating a three-part wall hanging. (1) Color and

> Review Enrichment Activity 2 (page 74) in the *Primary 7 New Testament Manual.*

cut out each piece. (2) Punch holes where indicated and at the top and bottom of each piece. (3) Tie ribbon or yarn to connect each piece, and a loop at the top to hang. (4) Ask children to look up the scriptures and fill in the blanks to learn how we can be merciful and forgiving. • *Scripture Challenge:* See details on page 93 (card on page 104).

THOUGHT TREAT (when appropriate): "M" and "F" Shaped Cookies or Bread. Roll out cookie dough or bread into thin ropes and shape into "M" and "F" letters. Bake and share one of each to children. Talk about being "M"erciful and "F"orgiving as Jesus was.

Jesus healed 10 lepers and only one returned to say

Thank you!

Can you name 10 things you could thank Jesus for?

fold

1. _____
2. _____
3. _____
4. _____
5. _____

fold

6. _____
7. _____
8. _____
9. _____
10. _____

I can ○ be...
MERCIFUL and FORGIVING

My _____, in days of old, sought occasion _____ one another and _____ not one another in their _____; and for this they were _____ and sorely _____.

D&C 64:8

Wherefore, I say unto _____, that ye ought to _____ one _____; for he that _____ not his _____ his trespasses standeth condemned before the _____; for there remaineth in him the _____ sin.

D&C 64:9

I, the _____, will _____ whom I will _____, but of _____ it is _____ to _____ all men.

D&C 64:10

Lesson 23 — Good Shepherd: I Will Follow Jesus

(Bite-size Memorize and Footstep Flash Cards Match Game)

John 10:4

Jesus is the good shepherd. I am his sheep. I will follow him.

YOU'LL NEED: *Copy of *Bite-size Memorize Stand-up Card* (shown left/page 44), two sets of *Footstep Flash Cards* (pages 45–46), and *Scripture Challenge Card* 23 (page 105) on cardstock paper for each child; scissors and markers.

Review Enrichment Activity #1 (page 77) in the *Primary 7 New Testament Manual*.

ACTIVITIES: · *Stand-up Card:* Children will be reminded to trust in Jesus as our Good Shepherd in creating this stand-up card. The card will help them memorize John 10:11, and know to read John 10:4. · *Footstep Flash Card Match Game:* (1) Review *Footstep Flash Cards* 1–12 with children, focusing on #8, "Jesus is Our Shepherd." Tell children that Jesus wants us to follow in His footsteps because He knows the way to eternal happiness. (2) Lay two sets of *Footstep Flash Cards* 1–12 facedown on a table or floor. (3) Play a match game by dividing children into two teams, taking turns turning cards over to make a match. The team with the most matches wins. · *Scripture Challenge:* See details on page 93 (card on p. 105).

THOUGHT TREAT (when appropriate): In His Steps Fudge. Make some instant fudge: add 2 bags of sweetened chocolate chips with 1 can sweetened and condensed milk and 1 teaspoon vanilla. Melt 12 minutes in the microwave, form into balls and then feet, pressing in candy toes. Treat reminds us to walk in the steps of Jesus.

Lesson 24 — Tithes and Offerings: I Will Build Up the Kingdom of God

(Windows of Heaven Bite-size Memorize)

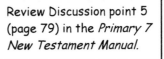

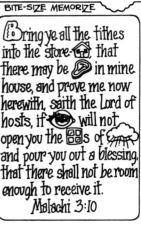

BITE-SIZE MEMORIZE

Bring ye all the tithes into the store-🏠, that there may be 🍖 in mine house, and prove me now herewith, saith the Lord of hosts, if 👁 will not open you the 🪟s of ☁, and pour you out a blessing, that there shall not be room enough to receive it. Malachi 3:10

YOU'LL NEED: *Copy of the *Bite-size Memorize* (page 47) and Scripture Challenge Card 24 (page 105) for each child; and markers.

ACTIVITY: · *Bite-size Memorize:* Help children learn why the Lord asks us to pay tithing, and the blessings that come from paying a full tithing as they look up and memorize Malachi 3:10 (also found in 3 Nephi 24:10). Fill in the blanks to learn how the windows of heaven will open to us and pour out blessings as we pay our tithes and offerings. · *Scripture Challenge:* See details on page 93 (card on page 105).

Review Discussion point 5 (page 79) in the *Primary 7 New Testament Manual*.

THOUGHT TREAT (when appropriate): Window Cookies. Frost graham crackers to look like windows. Tell children that as they bring their tithes and offerings into the house of the Lord (paying the bishop), they will begin to see blessings in their life. As we build up the kingdom of God, Heavenly Father will bless us daily.

John 10:4

Jesus is the good shepherd.
I am his sheep.
I will follow him.

I am the good shepherd:
the good shepherd giveth
his life for the sheep.
John 10:11

Bring ye all the tithes into the store-🏠, that there may be 🥩 in mine house, and prove me now herewith, saith the Lord of hosts, if 👁 will not open you the 🪟s of ⛈ and pour you out a blessing, that there shall not be room enough to receive it.

Malachi 3:10

Lesson 25 Second Coming: I Will Prepare to See Jesus
(Be Prepared Board Game)

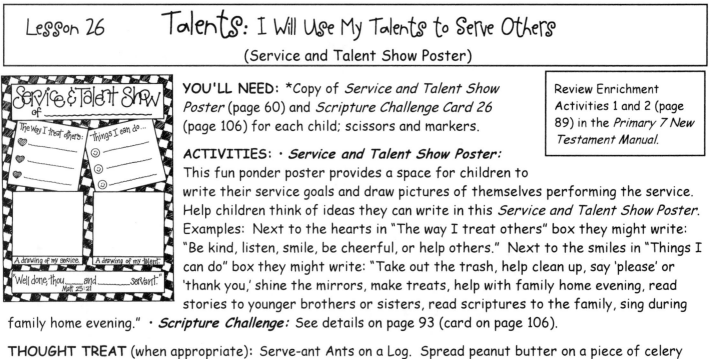

YOU'LL NEED: Copy of *Be Prepared Board Game* and wordstrips (pages 49-50) and *Scripture Challenge Card 25* (page 106) for each child; scissors, two coin markers, and markers.

Review Enrichment Activity 1-3 (pages 85-86) in the *Primary 7 New Testament Manual.*

ACTIVITIES: • *Be Prepared Board Game:* Discuss the second coming, President Kimball's ideas (2 and 3 in the lesson) on providing oil for our lamps, "drop by drop in righteous living," and the five virgins who were ready for the great day the bridegroom (Jesus) came.
Do Ahead: (1) *Color game board and cut out wordstrips. (2) Place wordstrips in a container. (3) Provide 2 different coins for markers.
To Play Game: (1) Divide class into two teams, giving each team a coin to place at START. (2) Teams take turns drawing and reading a wordstrip aloud. (3) Follow instructions, e.g., "move one", "move back," "lose a turn." (4) The first team to make it to Second Coming wins!
• *Scripture Challenge:* See details on page 93 (card on p. 106).

THOUGHT TREAT (when appropriate): Second Helping of Second Coming Mints. Give children a few mints and talk about the Second Coming of Jesus. Say, "Jesus 'mint' for all of us to live with Heavenly Father again." Give children a second helping of mints and say, "He wants us to prepare for His coming so we can have the blessings of eternal life. We don't know when He will come, so let's try each day to live the commandments so we will be ready."

Lesson 26 Talents: I Will Use My Talents to Serve Others
(Service and Talent Show Poster)

YOU'LL NEED: *Copy of *Service and Talent Show Poster* (page 60) and *Scripture Challenge Card 26* (page 106) for each child; scissors and markers.

Review Enrichment Activities 1 and 2 (page 89) in the *Primary 7 New Testament Manual.*

ACTIVITIES: • *Service and Talent Show Poster:*
This fun ponder poster provides a space for children to write their service goals and draw pictures of themselves performing the service. Help children think of ideas they can write in this *Service and Talent Show Poster.* Examples: Next to the hearts in "The way I treat others" box they might write: "Be kind, listen, smile, be cheerful, or help others." Next to the smiles in "Things I can do" box they might write: "Take out the trash, help clean up, say 'please' or 'thank you,' shine the mirrors, make treats, help with family home evening, read stories to younger brothers or sisters, read scriptures to the family, sing during family home evening." • *Scripture Challenge:* See details on page 93 (card on page 106).

THOUGHT TREAT (when appropriate): Serve-ant Ants on a Log. Spread peanut butter on a piece of celery and top with raisins (for ants). Tell children that we can be a serve-ant each day by developing our talents and using our talents to help others. If we don't use our talents, we may lose them. We should set goals each day and work on to increase them, like the ants who build an entire ant hill one step at a time.

You went to church. Move Ahead 3 Spaces.	You slept in and missed Primary. Move Back 1.	You read the Book of Mormon 20 minutes. Move Ahead 2.
You watched too much TV and didn't read your scriptures. Move Back 3.	You called your parents to tell them you would be late. Move Ahead 1.	You went to a friend's house and didn't call home. Move Back 2.
You tried to sing every song during Primary. Move Ahead 3.	You read your scriptures each day for a month. Move Ahead 2.	You didn't write in your journal all year. Lose Next Turn.
You read the prophet's message in the *Ensign*. Take Another Turn.	During the sacrament you thought about Jesus. Move Ahead 1.	You thought about your soccer game during the sacrament. Move Back 1.
You spent money all year and didn't save for your mission. Lose a Turn.	You forgot to watch general conference. Move Back 2.	You told a friend about our church. Move Ahead 3.
You read the story about Jesus blessing the children. Move Ahead 1.	You had the pioneer spirit and helped plant a garden. Move Ahead 1.	You helped your family bottle peaches. Move Ahead 1.
You kept the commandments when tempted to choose wrong. Move Ahead 3.	You asked your little brother to lie for you. Move Back 2.	You read the entire book of 1 Nephi. Take Another Turn.
You listened carefully to the family prayer. Move Ahead 2.	You fell asleep during family prayer. Move Back 1.	You have free agency and choose the right. Move Ahead 1.
You tended brother while Mom and Dad went to the temple. Move Ahead 1.	You promised yourself you would marry in the temple. Move Ahead 2.	You visited the temple grounds or a sacred place and prayed. Move Ahead 1.
Your mother had to ask you three times to help. Move Back 1.	You saw someone needed you and you didn't help. Move Back 2.	You woke up early each day for a week to read scriptures. Move Ahead 2.
You fed and played with your pet. Move Ahead 1.	You paid your tithing for one year and told the bishop. Move Ahead 1.	You cleaned your room without being asked. Take Another Turn.
You heard a bird sing, and thanked Heavenly Father. Move Ahead 1.	You gave your word you would keep the Word of Wisdom. Move Ahead 1.	You needed money, so you borrowed from your tithing. Move Back 1.
You fasted two meals on fast Sunday. Move Ahead 3.	You scrubbed the floor like Cinderella or Cinder-fella. Move Ahead 1.	You read a chapter in Proverbs for enjoyment. Move Ahead 1.
You wrote in your journal or family history book about you. Move Ahead 1.	You filled out a Family Group Sheet for your family history. Move Ahead 2.	You did your work without complaint for one week. Move Ahead 2.
You prayed with faith that Heavenly Father would help you. Move Ahead 1.	You forgot to thank your mother for a nice dinner. Move Back 1.	You helped plan and give family home evening. Move Ahead 2.
You sang the song, "Search, Ponder, and Pray." Move Ahead 1.	You were asked to cheat on a test at school and said "no." Move Ahead 1.	You didn't try to be reverent in class and others couldn't hear. Move Back 1.
You popped popcorn and sang, "Popcorn Popping." Move Ahead 1.	You sang, "I Have Two Little Hands," to your little sister. Move Ahead 1.	You said "no" to temptation. Move Ahead 1.
You forgot your mother's birthday and didn't help her. Move Back 1	You listened to the still small voice of the Holy Ghost. Move Ahead 1.	You wrote your grandmother and grandfather a letter. Move Ahead 1.
You thanked your teacher for a great lesson. Move Ahead 2.	You were assigned a talk in Primary and you didn't prepare. Move Back 1.	You felt you should do something good but didn't do it. Move Back 1.
You didn't cheer up the lonely or visit the elderly. Move Back 1.	You didn't obey your father when he called. Move Back 1.	Your motto is to "Choose the right to keep heaven in sight." Move Ahead 1.
You worked on Saturday to get ready for Sunday. Move Ahead 2.	You memorized the 13 Articles of Faith. Move Ahead 2.	You go to your parents or leaders when you have a problem. Move Ahead 1.
You raked your neighbor's leaves. Move Ahead 1.	You helped a little Sunbeam get a drink at the fountain. Move Ahead 1.	You raised your hand when you wanted to speak. Move Ahead 1.

Service & Talent Show

of _____

The Way I treat others:

♥ _____

♥ _____

♥ _____

Things I can do...

☺ _____

☺ _____

☺ _____

A drawing of my service.

A drawing of my talent.

"Well done, thou _____ and _____ servant."
Matt. 25:21

Lesson 27 — Service: Parable of the Sheep and Goats
(Sheep and Goat Situation Slap Game)

YOU'LL NEED: *Copy of *Sheep and Goat Situation Slap Game* (pages 53–54) and *Scripture Challenge Card 27* (page 107) on cardstock paper for each child; scissors and markers.

ACTIVITIES: · *Sheep and Goat Situation Slap Game:* Help children learn to apply the Parable of the Sheep and the Goats found in Matthew 25:31–46 by playing the Sheep and Goat Situation Slap Game. Tell children that

Review Enrichment Activity 5 (page 93) in the *Primary 7 New Testament Manual.*

in the Parable of the Sheep and Goats, the sheep are the ones that sit on the right hand of God. By choosing the right and serving our Heavenly Father, we are choosing to one day live with him again in the kingdom of God. *To Make Game:* *Color slap pad, and cut up and place situation wordstrips in a container.

To Play: (1) Divide class into two teams. (2) Take turns having a player from each team stand or kneel at the slap pad placed on the table or floor. (3) The two players stand or kneel with their hands to their side, ready to slap the SHEEP or GOAT on the pad. (4) Children can take turns drawing and reading a situation wordstrip aloud but not giving the SHEEP or GOAT answer. (5) Players guess which situation is a SHEEP (good action), or the GOAT (bad action) by slapping their hand on the SHEEP or GOAT. The first to guess right receives a point for their team. Tell children that the SHEEP is placed on the right of the pad as the SHEEP symbolize those who choose the right. (6) The team with the most points wins! Then have everyone say, "Choose the right to keep heaven in sight."
· *Scripture Challenge:* See details on page 93 (card on p. 107).

THOUGHT TREAT (when appropriate): Choose the Right Cupcakes. Frost CTR on top of a frosted cookie.

Lesson 28 — Faith in Christ: Others Testify that Jesus Is God's Son
(Testimonies of Jesus Scripture Picture Match)

YOU'LL NEED: *Copy of *Testimonies of Jesus Scripture Picture Match* cards (pages 55–56) and Scripture Challenge Card 28 (page 107), and a plastic for each child; scissors and markers.

ACTIVITIES: · *Testimonies of Jesus Scripture Picture Match:* Help children learn events where someone witnessed that Jesus Christ is the Son of God. Follow the instructions (page 54) to make and play the game. Place match cards in a zip-close plastic bag, along with the "Testimonies of Jesus Christ" label and game rules. · *Scripture Challenge:* See page 107.

Review Enrichment Activities 2–3 (page 97) in the *Primary 7 New Testament Manual.*

THOUGHT TREAT (when appropriate): Bite-size Treats. Offer bite-size treats, e.g., grapes, small cookies, or crackers to children. As they bite into them say, "These bite-sized treats remind us to take a bite out of the scriptures daily. Each day, let's read the scriptures to learn of the events that testify of Jesus Christ. Then when Jesus comes again, you will know Him.

SHEEP

GOAT

Parable of the sheep & the goats.
Matt. 25:31-46

You let your friend have a cupcake right in his face. **GOAT**	You stopped to help a friend, but changed your mind. **GOAT**	You told your friend you couldn't help him, but changed your mind. **SHEEP**
You were invited to a party, and didn't let them know you were coming. **GOAT**	You told your mother you would be home early, but you forgot and came home late. **GOAT**	You were late getting home, but you called your mother to let her know. **SHEEP**
You were in the mood for a good movie, and didn't do your homework. **GOAT**	You didn't volunteer to help sister dry the dishes, but you dried them anyway. **SHEEP**	Your told your mother you would tend your little brother, and he got lost. **GOAT**
You told your father you would put air in his bike tire, but you forgot. When he hurried out to ride it, the tire was flat. **GOAT**	You told the missionaries you didn't know anyone who wanted to hear the gospel, but you thought about it and gave them a name of your friend. **SHEEP**	Your friend asked you about Primary, so you asked him if he wanted to go. **SHEEP**
You told Uncle Steve you would help him clean his garage, but you went roller skating instead. **GOAT**	You didn't want to hurt your grandmother's feelings, so you accepted her reward, then you didn't do the job. **GOAT**	You told a joke to cheer up a friend, but the joke was not a clean joke. **GOAT**
To keep your spiritual boat afloat, you promised to read the scriptures, but you went swimming instead. **GOAT**	You told your parents you would tend your sister while they went to the temple, but you stayed at your friend's house too long, so they couldn't go. **GOAT**	You didn't want to go to church because your hair looked dorky, but you went anyway. **SHEEP**
You volunteered to give a talk in Primary, and worked on it all week. You gave a great talk. **SHEEP**	You said you would help with family home evening, but got sick. You said, "Sorry." **SHEEP**	You woke up late for church, you rushed around and forgot your socks; you listened anyway. **SHEEP**
You told your mother you would practice piano every day this week. You tried very hard and kept your promise. **SHEEP**	Thanksgiving is a day to give thanks, right? You were stuffed, and you missed your favorite pie, but you said "Thanks," anyway. **SHEEP**	You looked under the bed and found the $10 bill dad lost. You needed the money, but you didn't hesitate; you gave it to him. **SHEEP**
Your friends said they wanted to leave your other friend behind. You said you would stay with him. **SHEEP**	You decided to tell your sick friend about a special assignment at school. You went towards his house but met another friend and forgot. **GOAT**	It's recess at school and you saw someone fall down. You were with your friends and you ran on by without helping. **GOAT**
Your friend asked you to skip school, and you said, "No, it's not cool!" **SHEEP**	You decided to tell your friend he had bad breath. You did, but while others weren't listening. **SHEEP**	Tithing is to be paid every week or month. You decided to pay it, but kept it in your drawer for a year. **GOAT**
You read about Nephi's courage, but you doubted that you could do it, so you didn't even try. **GOAT**	Tomorrow is the last day for a book report. You read and wrote a ton of words, and were prepared. **SHEEP**	You hesitated when you saw a hungry looking person down on his luck. Then you gave him five bucks. **SHEEP**
You don't complain when you have work to do; you dig right in and do it. **SHEEP**	The scriptures say not to hide your light under a bushel. You didn't choose the right and dimmed your light. **GOAT**	You want to live the gospel of Jesus Christ, so you look for others to serve with a smile. **SHEEP**
When it's Christmas time you are tempted to buy gifts for yourself, but you buy for others instead. **SHEEP**	You like to read your scriptures each day, but you didn't get up in time, and you forgot to pray. **GOAT**	Others say, "You've got a lot of nerve to serve, and serve, and serve." You say, "It's fun to get the job done." **SHEEP**
You wake up in the morning and think about saying your prayers, but you put off saying them and forget. **GOAT**	There was work to do, you promised too. You then forgot and didn't pull through. **GOAT**	Last year you were more often late than early. This year you set a goal to not be so slow. **SHEEP**

Testimonies of Jesus Christ

Picture - Scripture Match Game

TO MAKE MATCH GAME:
1. Color and cut out cards.
2. Look up scriptures and fill in the missing words, talking about the event. Look at the matching picture as you talk about the event.

TO PLAY MATCH GAME:
1. Mix and lay cards face down on the floor.
2. Divide into two teams sitting across from each other in a circle.
3. Take turns turning cards over to make a match. The team with the most matches wins! If every player has not had a turn, play the game again.

EVENT THAT TESTIFIES OF JESUS CHRIST:

Jesus Raised Lazarus from the

John 11:25

"Jesus said unto her, I am the

_ _ _ _ _ _ _ _ _ _ _ _ _,

and the _ _ _ _: he that

_ _ _ _ _ _ _ _ _ in me,

though he were _ _ _ _, yet shall he

_ _ _ _."

(Jesus was speaking to Martha, the sister of Lazarus)

EVENT THAT TESTIFIES OF JESUS CHRIST:

Jesus Was Born

Luke 2:11

"An angel said, Unto you is

_ _ _ _ this day in the city

of _ _ _ _ _ _ a _ _ _ _ _ _,

which is Christ the _ _ _ _."

EVENT THAT TESTIFIES OF JESUS CHRIST:

Jesus Was Baptized

Mark 1:11

"There was a _ _ _ _ _ from

heaven saying, "Thou art my

_ _ _ _ _ _ _ Son"; the

Spirit of God descended like a dove.

EVENT THAT TESTIFIES OF JESUS CHRIST:

Jesus Walked on the Water

Matthew 14:25-27, 32-33

"In the fourth watch of the night Jesus went unto them, __ __ __ __ __ __ __ on the __ __ __." Jesus' disciples on the ship said, "Of a truth thou art the __ __ __ of __ __ __."

EVENT THAT TESTIFIES OF JESUS CHRIST:

Jesus Healed a Man Born Blind

John 9:32, 35-38

"And [the man] said, __ __ __ __, I __ __ __ __ __ __ __ [you are the Son of God]. And he worshipped him."

EVENT THAT TESTIFIES OF JESUS CHRIST:

Peter Testified of Christ

Matthew 16:13-16

When Jesus asked his disciples who they thought he was, Peter said, "Thou art the __ __ __ __ __ __, the Son of the __ __ __ __ __ __ God."

EVENT THAT TESTIFIES OF JESUS CHRIST:

Joseph Smith Receives His First Vision

Joseph Smith—History 1:17

Heavenly Father said, "This is My __ __ __ __ __ __ __ Son. __ __ __ __ Him!"

Lesson 29   Sacrament: I Will Think of Jesus
(Testimony Building Blocks Puzzle)

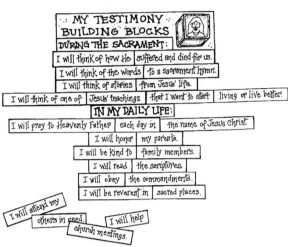

YOU'LL NEED: *Copy of *Testimony Building Blocks Word Puzzle* wordstrips (page 58) and *Scripture Challenge Card 29* (page 108) on cardstock paper, and a sheet of cardstock paper for each child; scissors, glue, and markers.

Review Enrichment Activity 3 (page 100) in the *Primary 7 New Testament Manual*.

ACTIVITIES: · *Testimony Building Blocks Word Puzzle:* Help children discover ways they can remember Jesus during the sacrament and in their daily life. Ask children to: (1) Cut out the wordstrips and mix them up laying faceup on the floor. (2) Use the extra sheet of cardstock paper and place the words on the paper in the correct order. Then glue blocks on paper as shown above.

Order of My Testimony Building Blocks:
· *During The Sacrament:* I will think of how He suffered and died for us. I will think of the words to a sacrament hymn. I will think of stories from Jesus' life. I will think of one of Jesus' teachings that I want to start living or live better.
· *In My Daily Life:* I will pray to Heavenly Father each day in the name of Jesus Christ. I will honor my parents. I will be kind to family members. I will read the scriptures. I will obey the commandments. I will be reverent in sacred places. I will help others in need. I will attend my church meetings. · *Scripture Challenge:* See p. 108.

THOUGHT TREAT (when appropriate): 'S'acrament Cookie. Cut out cookie dough in a 3" x 1/4" shape. Cut the letter 'S' in each cookie before baking, or frost cookies and write the letter 'S' with a tube of frosting. Give each child a cookie and say, "The letter 'S' in this cookie reminds us that the 'S'acrament is a 'S'acred time each week that we remember the 'S'avior, who 'S'acrificed his live for us."

Lesson 30   Repentance: Jesus Helped Me Overcome Sin and Death
(Repentance Puzzle)

YOU'LL NEED: *Copy of *Repentance Puzzle* (page 59) and *Scripture Challenge Card 30* (page 108) for each child; pencils and markers.

ACTIVITIES: · *Repentance Puzzle:* Read Mosiah 14:35 and Alma 7:11-12. Tell children that when Jesus suffered in the Garden of Gethsemane, He helped us overcome sin by suffering for our sins. This makes it possible for us to repent and be forgiven. He also suffered death, which makes it possible for us to live again. (1) *Color puzzle. (2) Fill in the puzzle using the words in the statement below.
· *Scripture Challenge:* See details on page 93 (card on page 108).

Review Enrichment Activity 3 (page 104) in the *Primary 7 New Testament Manual*.

THOUGHT TREAT (when appropriate): Repentance Rollups. Have each child roll out a red fruit rollup as you say, "Jesus rolled out the red carpet for us, giving us the royal treatment when He suffered for our sins. We are His sons and daughters, princes and princesses in His kingdom. If we repent and follow the straight and narrow path (carpet), we can return to our heavenly home."

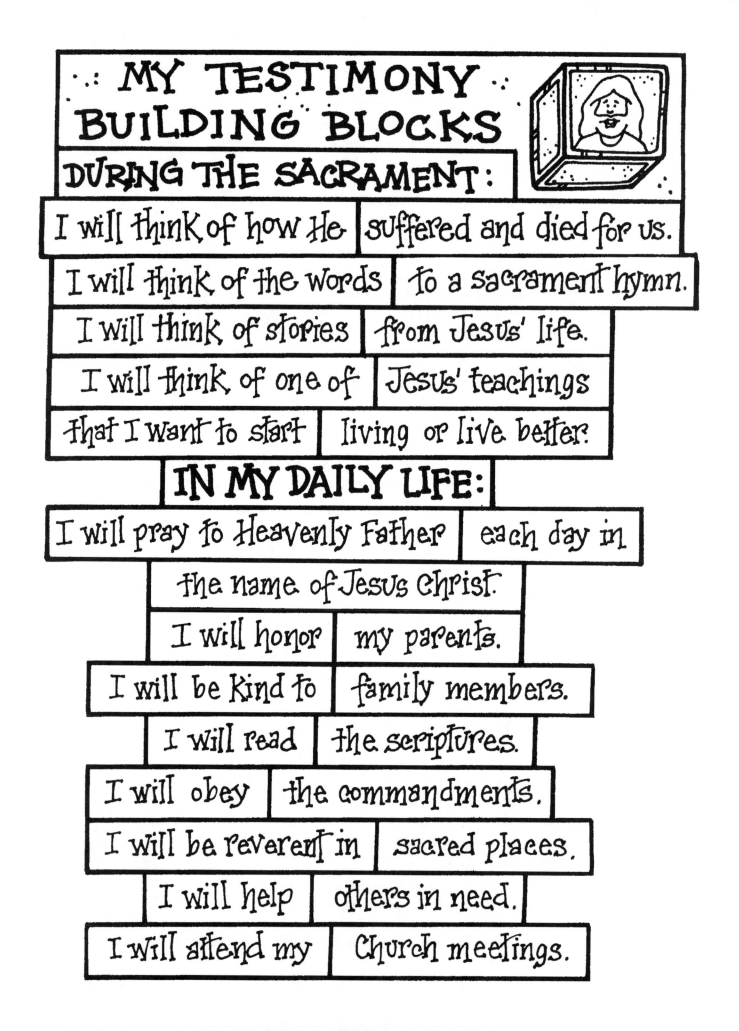

REPENTANCE

Jesus made it possible for me to repent!

✶ Find all the words in the special message below mixed-up in the puzzle!

Because Jesus suffered for my sins in the Garden of Gethsemane, I will repent and live the gospel of Jesus Christ.

Lesson 31 | Atonement: Jesus Is Our Life Savior
(Captain of Our Ship Show-and-tell Presentation)

YOU'LL NEED: *Copy of *Show-and-tell Pressentation* (pages 60-61), *Scripture Challenge Card 31* (page 108) on cardstock paper, and a file folder for each child; scissors, string, tape, flannel board, and markers. *Option:* Also copy this page (including the box below and file folder visual on the right) to give to children.

ACTIVITIES: • *Show-and-Tell Presentation:* Review the events in the final days of Jesus' earthly ministry using the following File Folder Family Home Evening show-and-tell presentation (taken from the book by Ross and Guymon-King *File Folder Family Home Evenings.* The children can do this in class and then present it in family home evening. (1) *Color and cut out visuals and the 1-6 cue cards. (2) Give each child a cue card with visuals to match the picture shown on the card. Images can be placed on a file folder with tape or sticky-back Velcro. *Option:* Punch holes and tie strings from ship to life preservers. (3) Before children help you with this presentation in class, read the following introduction in the box below.

> Review Attention Activity (page 105) in the *Primary 7 New Testament Manual.*

• *Scripture Challenge:* See details on page 93 (card on page 108).

THOUGHT TREAT (when appropriate): Save Our Ship Doughnuts. Tie red licorice string around a cake doughnut for each child to eat. Say, "Jesus is Our Life Savior. He is the captain of our ship. If we are to sail safely through the storms of life, we must hold onto the life preserver promises we made at baptism (see the Enrichment Activity 1, page 99 in the *Primary 7 New Testament* manual.)

CAPTAIN OF OUR SHIP

INTRODUCTION: Show a picture of Jesus and say: "Jesus is our LIFE SAVIOR. He is God's Son, and He knows His way back to our heavenly home.

Jesus taught us how to live Heavenly Father's commandments. With His teachings we can keep our spiritual boat afloat.

Jesus asked Heavenly Father to forgive us of our sins if we repent. He died for us and was resurrected so that we might live again. If you don't want to sink, follow the teachings of Jesus. He will bring you safely home.

We have a map for our journey through life. This map is found in the scriptures. The scriptures are the iron rod, or the word of God, that will guide us through life. Read the scriptures daily to stay on the lifeboat the Lord has provided."

#1   CAPTAIN OF OUR SHIP: Jesus Is Our Life Savior:

Jesus is our Life Savior. As we sail the sea of life, He is the captain of our ship. We can be protected against evil as we read the scriptures and learn of his teachings. We can sail safely to our heavenly home as we obey his commandments. He has shown us the way back.

Jesus Enters Jerusalem, and Pharisees Plot to Kill Him:

The disciples of Jesus did not want him to go to Jerusalem. They knew that the chief priests and Pharisees wanted to kill him. As they entered Jerusalem, the people cried out, *"Blessed is the King of Israel that cometh in the name of the Lord"* (John 12:12-13).

Jesus wants us to have faith in Him and know that His death was for a purpose. He had the power to save His own life, but He knew He had to go to Jerusalem to suffer, bleed, and die for us.

JESUS IS OUR LIFE SAVIOR.

#2   <u>Jesus and Apostles: Sacrament and Last Supper</u>:   Jesus and His apostles needed a place to eat the Passover dinner. Jesus sent Peter and John to look for a room. The Passover feast was to remind the Israelites that God saved them from Egyptian slavery with the help of Moses.

After the Passover feast, Jesus gave His apostles the first sacrament. He broke bread and blessed it. He told His apostles to eat this bread and always remember Him, that He would die for them.

Jesus poured some wine into a cup and blessed it, and told the apostles to drink it and remember Him. This was to remind them of the blood He would shed for them. He would bleed and suffer to take away the people's sins.

Jesus told them that wicked men would kill Him. This made the apostles sad, for they loved Jesus. Jesus knew that Judas would tell the wicked men where He was. Judas was one of his apostles.

Jesus wants us to remember Him each week as we partake of the sacrament. As we eat the bread, we are to remember that He allowed His body to be slain, and as we drink the water, we are to remember that His blood was shed. He suffered and died for our sins. The sacrament is very sacred and special.

#3   <u>Jesus Suffers for Our Sins in the Garden of Gethsemane</u>:   Jesus and the apostles went to the Garden of Gethsemane to pray. He asked Peter, James, and John to wait while He prayed. He prayed for a long time, and the apostles fell asleep.

While Jesus prayed, He suffered greatly for the sins of all the people in the world. He suffered for all those who lived before Him and who would live after Him.

He went back to Peter, James, and John several times and found them sleeping. He went back to pray again and again. He asked them to stay awake.

He continued to pray, and suffered so much that blood came out of his skin. He shook with sorrow for the sins of the world. An angel came to help Jesus through this.

When His suffering was finally over, He came back and found Peter, James, and John sleeping. He told them that wicked men were coming to kill Him.

Jesus wants us to remember that He suffered for our sins. He wants us to live a righteous life. If we do sin, He wants us to repent, pray, and ask for forgiveness. Then He wants us to choose the right.

#4 <u>**Jesus Is Crucified and He Forgives His Enemies**</u>: Wicked men were sent by the Pharisees to take Jesus as a prisoner. They came into the garden with sticks and swords. Judas kissed Jesus to show the wicked men who Jesus was. The Pharisees paid Him for finding Jesus.

The Pharisees took Jesus to Pilate, the Roman leader in Jerusalem. Pilate told the Pharisees Jesus had done nothing wrong. The Pharisees demanded Jesus' crucifixion. Pilate did not want trouble with the Pharisees, so He let his soldiers crucify Jesus.

The soldiers took Jesus and beat Him with whips, and made fun of Him. They made a crown of thorns and pressed it down on His head, which made His head bleed. They took Him to a hill near Jerusalem, laid Him on a wooden cross, and nailed His hands and feet to the cross. Then they lifted up the cross, causing Him great pain.

Jesus prayed that Heavenly Father would forgive the soldiers who crucified Him, for they did not know He was the Savior. Jesus asked the apostle John to take care of His mother.

Jesus suffered for many hours, then He died. His spirit left His body. The sky became dark, and there was a great earthquake. The soldiers were afraid. One of the apostles took Jesus' body, wrapped it in cloth, and placed it in a tomb. A large rock was placed in front of the tomb.

#5 <u>**Jesus Is Resurrected: He Is Our Life Savior**</u>: After the body of Jesus was in the tomb three days, two angels came and moved the rock away. This was on a Sunday morning.

A friend of Jesus, Mary Magdalene, came to the tomb. She saw that the body of Jesus was gone. She ran to tell the apostles Peter and John. They came and saw the cloth that He was buried in. Then they rushed home.

Mary stayed at the tomb, crying. As she looked in the tomb, she saw two angels. The angels asked her why she was crying. She told them someone had taken away the body of Jesus.

Mary turned around and saw Jesus standing there. She thought He was the gardener. Jesus said, *"Mary."* Then she knew He was Jesus. He asked her to go tell the apostles He had been resurrected. She ran and told the apostles, but they did not believe her.

Later, Jesus came to the apostles. They were afraid, thinking Jesus was dead. Jesus asked them why they were afraid. He ask them to touch His hands and feet and feel the nail prints. They could see that Jesus was resurrected. He was alive again. His body and spirit had come together. The apostles were happy to see Jesus. They ate fish and honey with Him.

As Jesus was the first person to be resurrected, all other people will be resurrected, too.

#6 <u>**Jesus Says Farewell and Sends the Holy Ghost**</u>: After Jesus was resurrected, He stayed with the apostles 40 days. He taught them about His church, and asked them to teach the gospel to all the people.

He said that He would leave soon, but He would send a comforter to guide and help them. This comforter would be the Holy Ghost.

Then Jesus went to Heavenly Father. As the apostles watched Him ascend up to heaven, two men came down in white clothes. They stood by the apostles, saying that Jesus would come back someday. When He did come back, He would come out of heaven.

The apostles were now the leaders of the church. Judas was dead, so there were only 11 apostles. They chose Matthias to be the 12th apostle. The apostles held the priesthood and continued to teach the people and heal the sick. They were missionaries. People believed the teachings about Jesus, and joined His church. They were called saints.

Jesus is our LIFE SAVIOR. He is the captain of our ship. If we are to sail safely to our heavenly home, we must do as He taught. Jesus wants us to follow in His steps—to pray often, read the scriptures, be baptized, be faithful members of His church, repent, learn of His miracles, live His parables, and teach others His gospel. This way we can live with Heavenly Father again.

Jesus and Apostles

Jesus Suffers For Our Sins

Jesus Is Crucified

Lesson 32 — Atonement: Jesus Suffered for Me
(Atonement Ponder Wheel)

YOU'LL NEED: *Copy of *Atonement Ponder Wheel* (pages 67-68) and *Scripture Challenge Card 32* (page 109) on cardstock, a paper fastener (brad) for each child; scissors, razor blade (option), and markers.

ACTIVITIES: • *Atonement Ponder Wheel:* Create a crucifixion wheel to show what Jesus said while hanging on the cross. These statements tell of the power and character of Jesus that helped Him to say and do these things. Have children take turns reading and discuss the statements Jesus made, e.g., Luke 23:34 says that Jesus was "merciful and forgiving." (1) *Color and cut out wheel parts A and B and scripture window (from part A) with scissors or a razor blade (ahead of time). (2) Place a metal brad in the center and turn wheel.

> Review Enrichment Activity 1 (page 111) in the *Primary 7 New Testament Manual.*

• *Scripture Challenge:* See details on page 93 (card on page 109).

THOUGHT TREAT (when appropriate): Crucifixion Wheel Cookies. Roll out sugar cookie dough and cut into a 4" round shape. Then cut dividing lines in cookie before baking (to show the six parts on the wheel like the crucifixion wheel above). As children eat each piece of the wheel cookie, talk about the six points on the wheel that describe Jesus.

Lesson 33 — Resurrection: Jesus Gave Everyone a New Beginning
(Flower Pot Quiz)

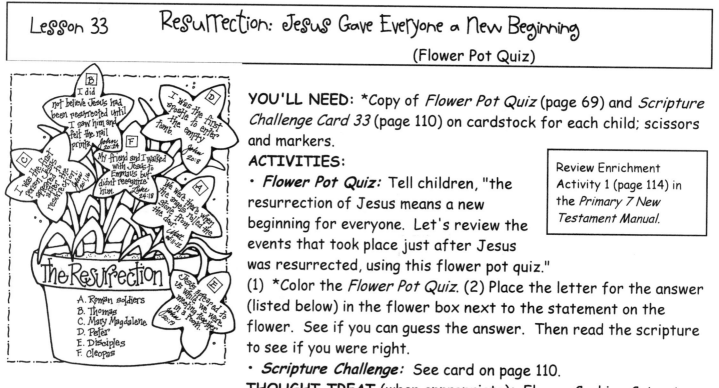

YOU'LL NEED: *Copy of *Flower Pot Quiz* (page 69) and *Scripture Challenge Card 33* (page 110) on cardstock for each child; scissors and markers.

ACTIVITIES:

• *Flower Pot Quiz:* Tell children, "the resurrection of Jesus means a new beginning for everyone. Let's review the events that took place just after Jesus was resurrected, using this flower pot quiz."

> Review Enrichment Activity 1 (page 114) in the *Primary 7 New Testament Manual.*

(1) *Color the *Flower Pot Quiz*. (2) Place the letter for the answer (listed below) in the flower box next to the statement on the flower. See if you can guess the answer. Then read the scripture to see if you were right.

• *Scripture Challenge:* See card on page 110.

THOUGHT TREAT (when appropriate): Flower Cookie. Cut out sugar cookies into flower shapes and bake. Frost and add a gumdrop in the center.

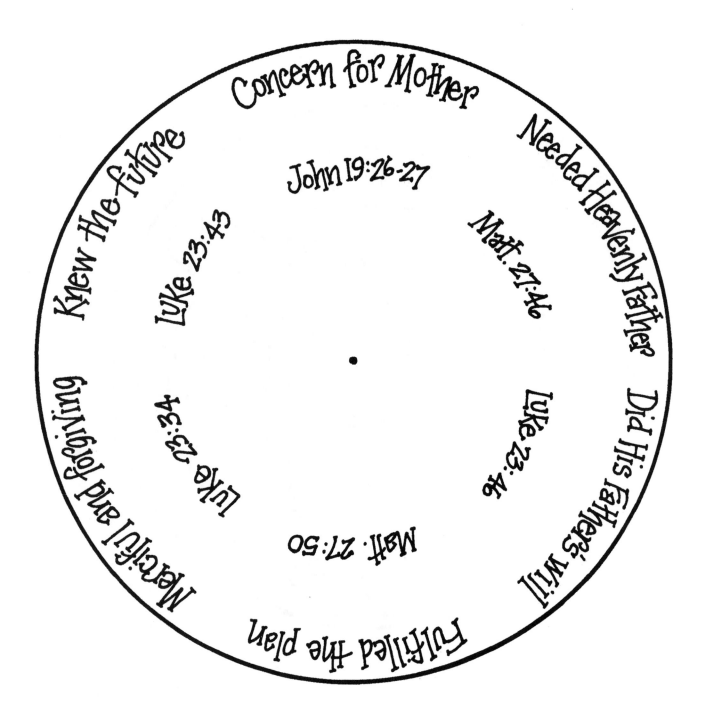

Concern for Mother

Needed Heavenly Father

Knew the future

John 19:26-27

Matt. 27:46

Luke 23:43

Did His Father's will

Merciful and forgiving

Luke 23:34

Luke 23:46

Matt. 27:50

Fulfilled the plan

I did not believe Jesus had been resurrected until I saw him and felt the nail prints. John 20:24

I was the first apostle to enter the empty tomb. John 20:8

I was the first person Jesus appeared to after the resurrection. John 20:1,16

My friend and I walked with Jesus to Emmaus but didn't recognize him. Luke 24:18

We were there when the angels rolled the stone from the door. Matt. 28:11-12

The Resurrection

A. Roman soldiers
B. Thomas
C. Mary Magdalene
D. Peter
E. Disciples
F. Cleopas

Jesus appeared to us while we were meeting together in a room. John 20:19

Lesson 34   **Service:** I Will Follow Jesus and Feed His Sheep

(Service Origami Game)

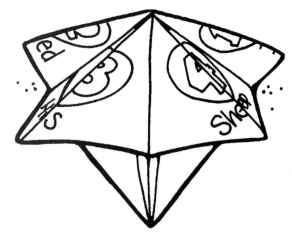

YOU'LL NEED: *Copy of *Service Origami Game* (page 71), game rules (below), and *Scripture Challenge Card 34* (page 110) for each child; chalk and eraser or paper and pencil (to keep score), and markers.

ACTIVITIES: • *Service Origami Game:* Play this fun origami finger game to find key words and tell how children can show love and service like Jesus did. *To Make Game:* Follow the steps/figures below.

> Review Enrichment Activity 1 (pages 117-118) in the *Primary 7 New Testament Manual.*

To Play the Game:

1. One person moves the origami game while others play. To hold, place fingers in fold pockets with the thumbs under the word "Feed" and "His."

2. Divide players into two teams.

3. Have someone keep score, writing "I Feed His Sheep" on the blackboard or create and display a sign.

4. Players take turns choosing one of the four words "I," "Feed," "His," or "Sheep."

5. The word chosen matches a number in the heart, which determines the number of moves.

Start folding with paper face down, blank side up.

1.

2.

Turn over so flaps are face down, numbers face up.

3.

4.

Example: If the word "I" was chosen, open the origami once, showing the words they chose. Choose a word and say something about the word. For example, if the word is "teach," tell others to teach by example. Then open the inside flap of the origami to see how many points their team receives.

6. Keep playing until time is up or until each person has had a turn. The team with the most points wins.

• *Scripture Challenge:* See details on page 93 (card on page 110).

THOUGHT TREAT (when appropriate): Sheep Food (popcorn to share). Tell children that corn is a food that sheep eat. Ask, "What did Jesus mean when he said, 'Feed my sheep'?" We nourish others with the gospel by loving and serving them. Open the origami game to review ways we can show love.

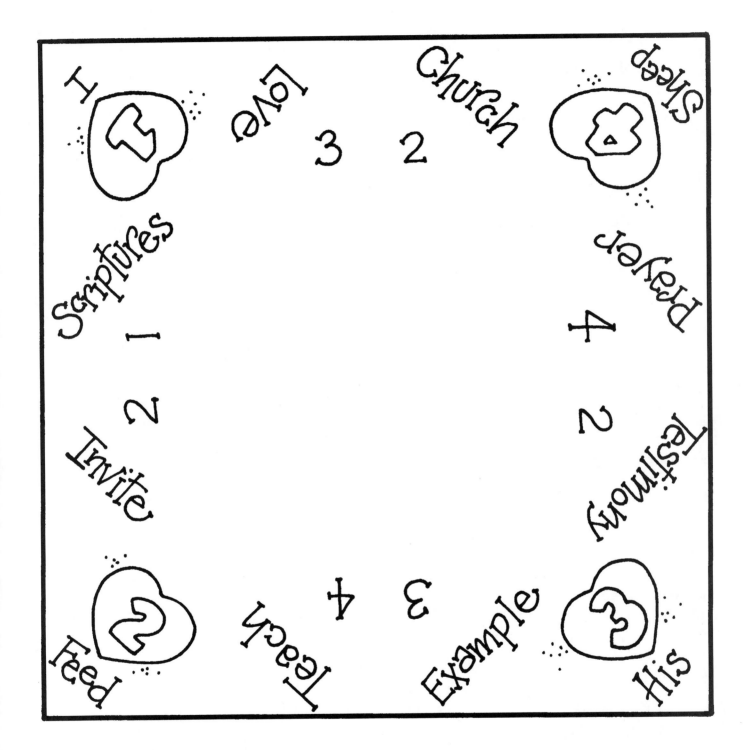

Lesson 35	Mission: The Mission of Jesus Christ
	(The Mission of Jesus Christ Review Game)

The Mission of **Jesus Christ**

Christ's Premortal Life

[3] Volunteered to ... be our Savior. [11] Created ... the earth. [14] Was Jehovah ... of the Old Testament. [16] Gave prophets ... revelation.

Christ's Mortal Life

[1] Taught ... the gospel. [6] Healed ... the sick. [7] Organized ... His Church. [12] Died that we ... might live again. [2] Atoned ... for our sins.

Christ's Life After Death

[5] Visited the ... spirit world. [15] Was ... resurrected. [9] Visited ... the Nephites. [13] Organized the ... Church through Joseph Smith. [4] Gives revelation ... to leaders today. [10] Loves and ... helps us. [8] Will come ... again.

YOU'LL NEED: *Copy of *The Mission of Jesus Christ Review Game* (pages 73-74), *Moses 1:39 Poster* (page 75), and Scripture Challenge Card 35 (page 111) for each child; scissors, tape, and markers.

ACTIVITIES: • *The Mission of Jesus Christ Review Game:* Read to children the mission statement Jesus Christ gave to Moses (Moses 1:39 on poster, page 74): *"Behold, this is my work and my glory—to bring to pass the immortality and eternal life of man."* Then play these review games to learn how Jesus fulfilled His mission before, during, and after His life on this Earth.

To Make Game: (1) *Color and cut out cards and wordstrips. (2) Place wordstrips on the board lengthwise so cards can be placed below wordstrips.

To Play Review Game: (1) Divide class into two teams. Give each team 8 cards with tape on the back (to mount on the wall). (2) Take turns placing the card under the matching wordstrip. If the match is correct, the team receives 10 points. The first team to win 100 points wins first game. *Answers:* Place the following numbered cards under the wordstrips: "Christ's Premortal Life" (3, 11, 14, 16) "Christ's Mortal Life" (1, 6, 7, 12, 2) "Christ's Life After Death" (5, 15, 9, 13, 4, 10, 8)
• *Scripture Challenge:* See details on page 93 (card on page 111).

Review Enrichment Activity 3 (page 122) in the *Primary 7 New Testament Manual.*

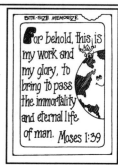

BITE-SIZE MEMORIZE

For behold, this is my work and my glory, to bring to pass the immortality and eternal life of man. Moses 1:39

THOUGHT TREAT (when appropriate): Something Sweet. Say that Jesus was sweet to show us all this love.

Lesson 36	Holy Ghost: The Comforter Will Teach Me All Things
	(John 14:26 Bite-size Memorize Poster)

BITE-SIZE MEMORIZE

But the [Comforter], which is the Holy Ghost whom the Father [will] send in my name, He shall teach [you] all things and bring all things 2 [you] remembr. John 14:26

YOU'LL NEED: *Copy of *Bite-size Memorize* (page 76) and Scripture Challenge Card 36 (page 111) for each child; scissors and markers.

ACTIVITIES: • *Bite-size Memorize:* Help children learn about the gift of the Holy Ghost by memorizing John 14:26. • *Scripture Challenge:* See page 111.

Review Enrichment Activity 2 and 5 (pages 125-126) in the *Primary 7 New Testament Manual.*

THOUGHT TREAT (when appropriate): Quilted Comforter Cookies. Say that the Holy Ghost is the comforter. He helps us feel warm inside when we choose the right.
To Make Cookie: Roll out sugar cookie dough 1/4" thick, and cut out 3" x 4" cookies. Cut quilt squares with a butter knife. Then paint squares with cookie paints before baking (mix 2 tsp. milk with food coloring).

BITE-SIZE MEMORIZE

For behold, this is my work and my glory, to bring to pass the immortality and eternal life of man. Moses 1:39

But the [comforter], which is the Holy Ghost whom the Father [sent] send in my name, He shall teach U all things and bring all things 2 UR remembr.

John 14:26

Lesson 37   Testimony: I Can "Bear" My Testimony!

(Find the Secret Message Poster)

YOU'LL NEED: *Copy of *Secret Message Poster* (page 78) and *Scripture Challenge Card 37* (page 112) on cardstock paper for each child; pencils and markers.

Poster: Let children discover the secret message on their own to learn what to say when they "bear" their testimony. (1) *Color poster. (2) Using the words in the message below, fill in the blanks. *Answers* (shown left: know, of, is, Jesus Christ, true, gospel, the).
• *Scripture Challenge:* See card on page 112.

Review Enrichment Activity 1 (page 129) in the *Primary 7 New Testament Manual.*

THOUGHT TREAT (when appropriate): Testimony Tarts. Serve tarts with berry filling and say, "A testimony is berry (very) sweet, just like this tart."

Lesson 38   Honesty: I Will Be Honest in Thought, Word, and Deed

(Drawing Honest and Dishonest Faces)

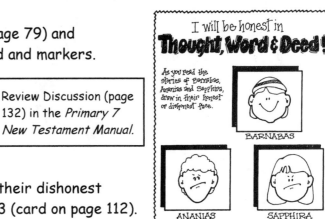

YOU'LL NEED: *Copy of *I Will Be Honest Poster* (page 79) and *Scripture Challenge Card 38* (page 112) for each child and markers.

ACTIVITIES: • *Drawing Honest and Dishonest Faces:* Tell children the story of Barnabas, Ananias, and Sapphira found in Acts 4:36–37; 5:1-2, 7-8. While children are listening to the story a second time, have them draw Barnabas with his honest face, and Ananias and Sapphira with their dishonest faces. • *Scripture Challenge:* See details on page 93 (card on page 112).

Review Discussion (page 132) in the *Primary 7 New Testament Manual.*

THOUGHT TREAT (when appropriate): Honest Face Pancake. These pancakes are served cold, but they leave children with a warm feeling. Color ½ cup pancake batter blue and ½ cup batter red, using a drop or two of food coloring in each. Make oval-shaped pancakes. After turning the pancake, pour two drops of blue batter for the eyes and a streak of red batter for the smile. Then turn pancake over for 30 seconds to cook facial features. As children eat smiling, honest face pancakes, talk about the happy feelings you receive when you are honest.

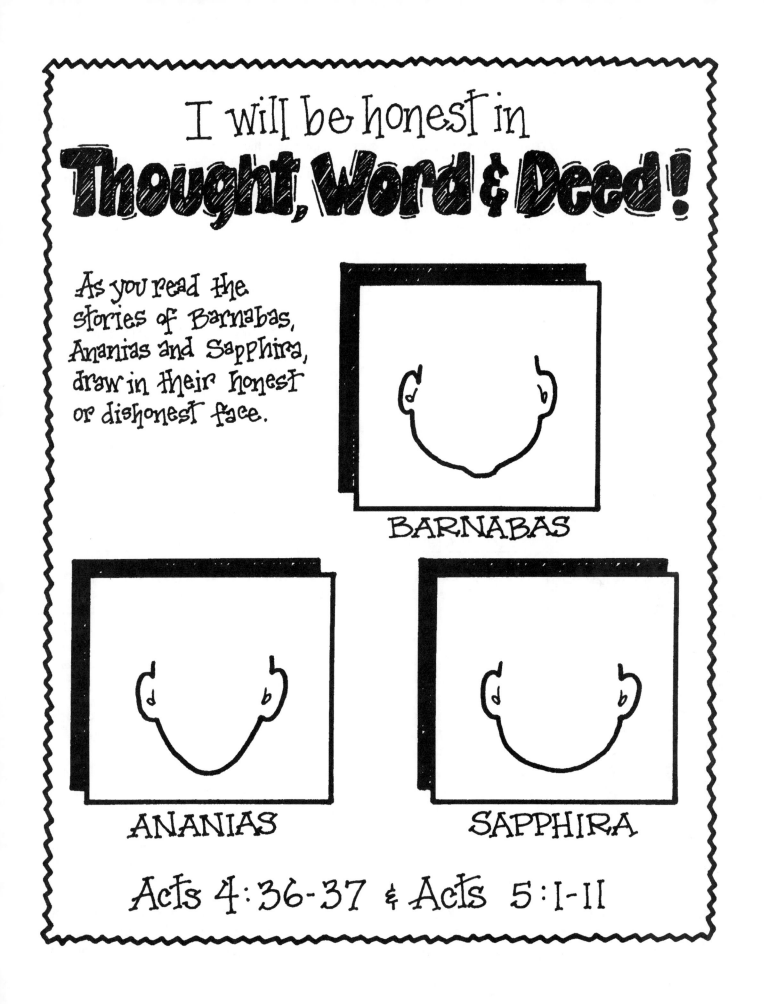

Lesson 39 Godhead: I Love Heavenly Father, Jesus Christ, and the Holy Ghost
(Godhead 3-D Teaching Tool)

YOU'LL NEED: *Copy of *Godhead 3-D Teaching Tool* (page 81) and *Scripture Challenge Card 39* (page 113) for each child; scissors, glue, and markers.

ACTIVITIES: • **Godhead 3-D Teaching Tool:** Help children create a teaching tool they can share with their nonmember friends to tell what we believe, reciting the first Article of Faith: *"We believe in God, the Eternal Father, and in His Son, Jesus Christ, and in the Holy Ghost."* To Make: (1) *Color and cut out card. (2) Fold on lines. (3) Bend back tab and glue to card. (4) Review card by having three children read the three sides of the stand up card. • **Scripture Challenge:** See page 93 and 113).

> Review Enrichment Activity 4 (page 137) in the *Primary 7 New Testament Manual.*

THOUGHT TREAT (when appropriate): Sunshine Cookie. Create a sunshine cookie made from a cake mix. Tell children that the sun is a special light Heavenly Father gave us to give warmth and light to the earth. The Godhead provides a special light to warm our spirit. Heavenly Father is known as God the Father, and Jesus Christ is God's Son. When you eat this sun cookie, think of the Son of God. The light of Christ dwells in every man, and the Holy Ghost is a special light we receive after we are baptized and confirmed a member of The Church of Jesus Christ of Latter-day Saints. *Sunshine Cookie:* Mix together an 18-ounce yellow cake mix, 3/4 cup water, and 2 eggs. Drop by tablespoonsful, three inches apart, onto a greased cookie sheet. Bake 8-11 minutes at 375°.

Lesson 40 Missionary: Heavenly Father Wants Everyone to Learn the Gospel
(My Mission Statement Message Decoder)

YOU'LL NEED: *Copy of *My Mission Statement Puzzle* (page 82) *Scripture Challenge Card 40* (page 113) for each child, pencils, and markers.

ACTIVITIES: • **My Mission Statement Message Decoder:** "We'll Bring the World His Truth" (page 172) in *Children's Songbook* (contains clues to the mission statement). (1) *Color page. (2) Help children learn how they

> Review Enrichment Activity 2 (page 141) in the *Primary 7 New Testament Manual.*

can be missionaries by printing the letters of the pictured objects to decode the message *"I will learn and teach the gospel of Jesus Christ."* (3) Tell children that Jesus Christ had to learn the gospel before He taught it. We too must learn all we can about the gospel of Jesus Christ. As we learn something about the gospel from our teachers and reading the scriptures, let's share what we learn with others. Sharing the gospel and living the gospel is the best way to gain and keep our testimony. Jesus' testimony grew each day because He learned about the gospel and shared His testimony with others. Our testimony can grow each day. We can "increase in wisdom" as Jesus did. Read Luke 2:52. (4) Do Scripture Challenge as detailed on page 93. • **Scripture Challenge:** See pages 93 and 113.

THOUGHT TREAT (when appropriate): Promise Peanut Butter Cookies. Make peanut butter cookies by rolling dough into a ball, pressing down with a Hershey's candy kiss (unwrapped), and bake. As children eat the cookie, and come to the big candy kiss, ask them to name one big thing they promise to do to prepare for their mission.

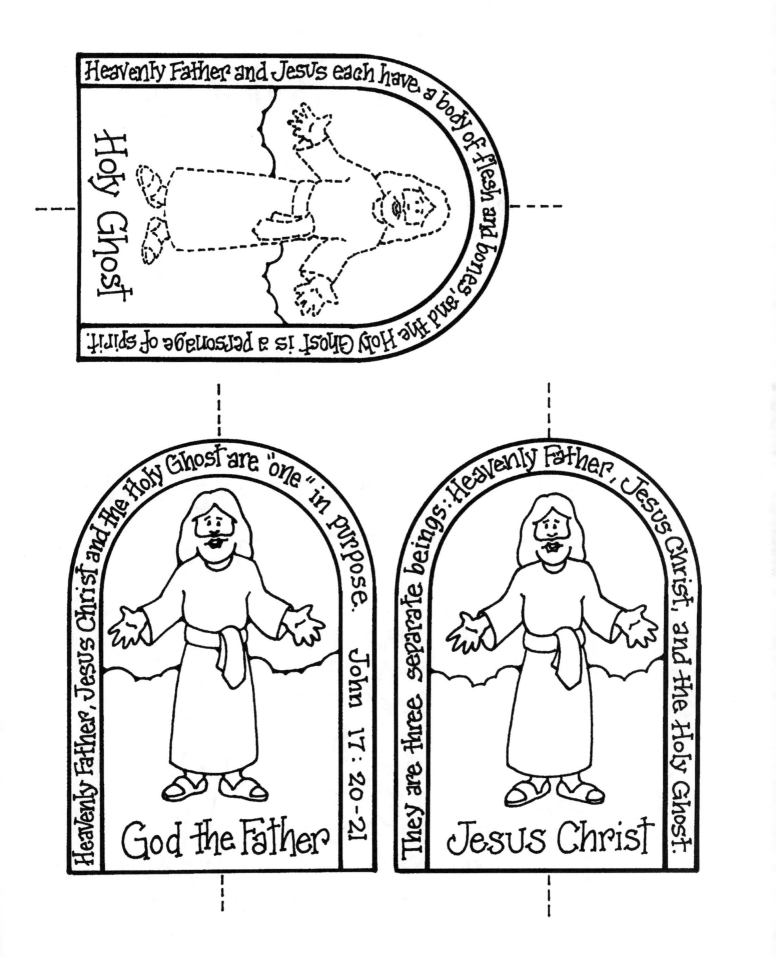

Heavenly Father and Jesus each have a body of flesh and bones, and the Holy Ghost is a personage of spirit.

Holy Ghost

Heavenly Father, Jesus Christ and the Holy Ghost are "one" in purpose. John 17: 20-21

God the Father

They are three separate beings: Heavenly Father, Jesus Christ, and the Holy Ghost.

Jesus Christ

My Mission Statement

To learn how you can be a missionary, print the letters of the pictured objects to decode the message.

Lesson 41	Speech: I Can Be Tongue Tight
	(Sweet Speech! Word Search)

YOU'LL NEED: *Copy of Sweet Speech! Word Search (page 84) and Scripture Challenge Card 41 (page 114) on cardstock for each child; scissors and markers.

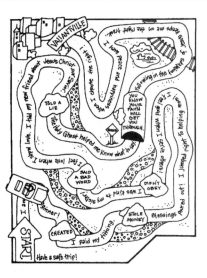

SWEET SPEECH Untwist these sour words to sweeten up your tongue!

ESEPLA	P L E A S E
KAHTNUYO	T H A N K Y O U
UYLIEVOO	I L O V E Y O U
ROSRY	S O R R Y
MROFVGIEE	F O R G I V E M E
ESEEUCXM	E X C U S E M E
BYULSESO	B L E S S Y O U

ACTIVITIES: · *Sweet Speech! Word Search:* Read and discuss Proverbs 23:7 and talk about ways to control tempers, e.g., counting to ten, singing a song, e.g., "Hum Your Favorite Hymn," page 152 in *Children's Songbook,* have cool-down words to replace the bad words. To learn how you can be tongue tight, to sweeten your speech: Untwist the words on the left and write them on the right. *Answers:* ESEPLA is "PLEASE," KAHTNUYO is "THANK YOU," UYLIEVOO is "I LOVE YOU," ROSRY is "SORRY,", MROFVGIEE is "FORGIVE ME," ESEEUCXM is "EXCUSE ME," and BYULSESO is "BLESS YOU."
· *Scripture Challenge:* See details on page 93 (card on page 114).

> Review Testimony (page 146) in the *Primary 7 New Testament Manual.*

THOUGHT TREAT (when appropriate): Sweet-and-Sour Speech Smarties. Give each child 7 Smartie treats (sweet and sour wrapped candy pills). As they eat them, think of the seven Sweet Speech words they can use to sweeten their tongue. Tell them that it is smart to choose sweet speech instead of sour speech. Give them some Smarties to take them home and eat one each time they practice sweet speech.

Lesson 42	Testimony: I Will Stay on the Right Road to Happiness
	(Valiantville "Convert"-able Obstacle Course)

YOU'LL NEED: *Copy of Valiantville Obstacle Course and car (page 85) and Scripture Challenge Card 42 (page 114) on colored cardstock paper for each child; scissors and markers. *Option:* Enlarge obstacle course to show in class.

ACTIVITY: · *Valiantville Obstacle Course:*
Talk to children about taking the right and wrong turns in life and where they might lead.
To Make: *Color obstacle course without coloring over words and cut out the car. *To Play Game:*
Take turns tossing a coin (heads = one sentence forward, tails = one sentence backward. The first team to get to Valiantville wins! *Travel Tips:* Travel through this obstacle course as a class or individually with your own private car. Cut out the car and go! As you start, you are on testimony trail. Try to move to Valiantville to find happiness. Valiantville is Zion, the city of eternal happiness. To take your journey, move your "convert"-able car as you go about getting converted. When an obstacle (big rock) comes, say "no" to temptation. To get back on the road, back out onto repentance road (the bumpy path). Remember that this road is not smooth. It can be rough to repent, but it is worth it to turn your life around. You will feel better when you are back on testimony trail.
· *Scripture Challenge:* See details on page 93 (card on page 114).

> Review Enrichment Activity 5 (page 149) in the *Primary 7 New Testament Manual.*

THOUGHT TREAT (when appropriate): Valiantville Graham Cracker Town. Frost graham crackers to make a village with a "Valiantville" sign. Children can eat the village once they have thought through the maze.

SWEET SPEECH

Untwist these sour words to sweeten up your tongue!

ESEPLA	_ _ _ _ _ _
KAHTNUYO	_ _ _ _ _ _ _ _
UYLIEVOO	_ _ _ _ _ _ _ _
ROSRY	_ _ _ _ _
MROFVGIEE	_ _ _ _ _ _ _ _ _
ESEEUCXM	_ _ _ _ _ _ _
BYULSESO	_ _ _ _ _ _ _ _

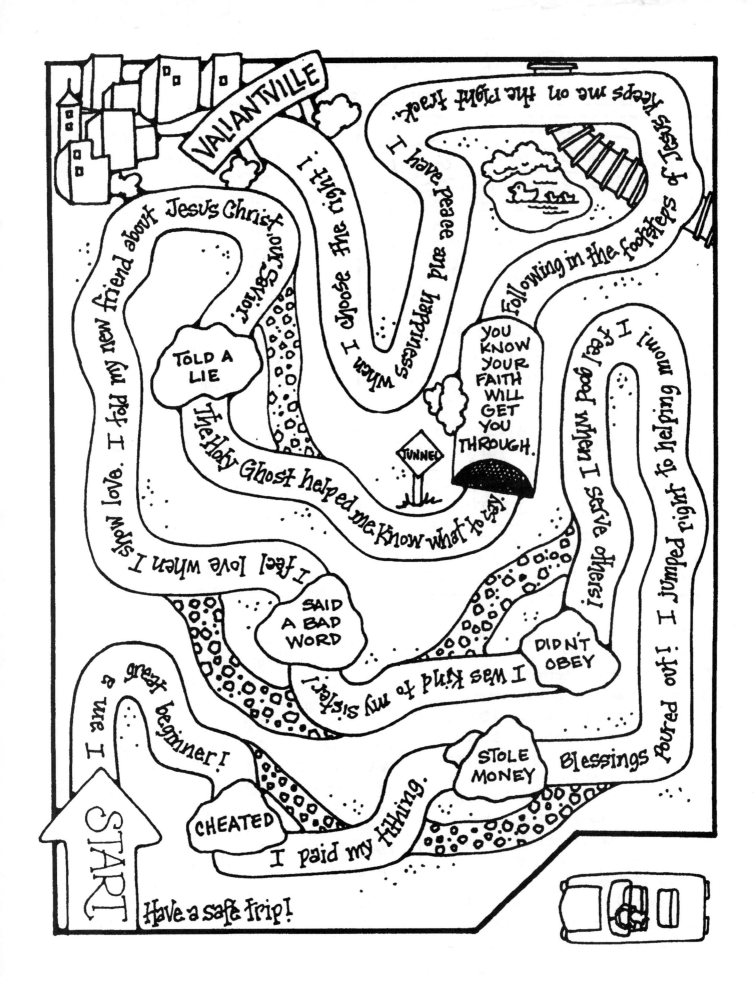

Lesson 43   Testimony: I Will Be Valiant and Testify of Jesus
(Valiant Testimony Balloon Maze)

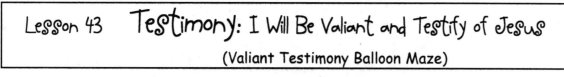

I will be valiant and testify of Jesus!
Find out what qualities are needed so our lives will testify of Jesus Christ.

PRE UGUO AO   FAITHFUL   NA ET PE N

COURAGEOUS

EOSN   TRUSTWORTHY

FAU IHT   PRAYERFUL   AF JU YE YR

VIRTUOUS   NE EDB I   HONEST

WR HSR UTT O   REPENTANT   RI UT OU

OBEDIENT

YOU'LL NEED: *Copy of *Valiant Testimony Balloon Maze* (page 86) and *Scripture Challenge Card 43* (page 115) for each child; pencils and markers.

> Review Attention Activity (page 151) and Enrichment Activity 2 (page 153) in the *Primary 7 New Testament Manual.*

ACTIVITIES: • *Valiant Testimony Balloon Maze:* Help children learn how they can acquire a valiant testimony that can help them testify of Jesus Christ and His plan of salvation. (1) *Color balloon maze. (2) Find the missing letters that go in the word box by drawing a line (with different colored crayons, pencils, or markers) to the balloon. (3) Unscramble missing letters and place them in the word box to learn ways you can be valiant.
• *Scripture Challenge:* See details on page 93 (card on page 115).

THOUGHT TREAT (when appropriate): Balloon Bite-size Cakes.
To Make: (1) Make a batter with 18-ounces of white or yellow cake mix, 3/4 cup of water, and 2 eggs. (2) Divide batter into four containers. (3) Drop a different food coloring, e.g., yellow, red, blue, green into batter. (4) Stir, and drop by tablespoonsful 2" apart onto a greased cookie sheet. (5) Place a two-inch licorice string in the bottom half of each. (6) Bake 8-11 minutes at 375°.
To Serve Balloon Cakes: As you eat balloon cakes, have children tell you how they can soar with a valiant testimony (using words on the balloon maze).

ANSWERS:
Matching Balloons Letters:
Completed Word in the Box:

FAUIHT	F A I T H F U L
REUGUOAO	C O U R A G E O U S
WRHSRUTTO	T R U S T W O R T H Y
AFYEURR	P R A Y E R F U L
RUOITU	V I R T U O U S
EOSN	H O N E S T
NAETPEN	R E P E N T A N T
NEEDBI	O B E D I E N T

I will be valiant and testify of Jesus!

Find out what qualities are needed so our lives will testify of Jesus Christ.

RE UGUO AO

F_____L

C_____S

NA ET PE N

EOSN

T_____Y

FAU IHT

P_____L

AF UJ YEU RR

V_____S

NE EDB I

H_____T

WR HSR UTT O

R_____T

RI UT OU

O_____T

Lesson 44   Missionary: I Will Prepare Now to Share the Gospel

(Missionary Mystery! Word Search)

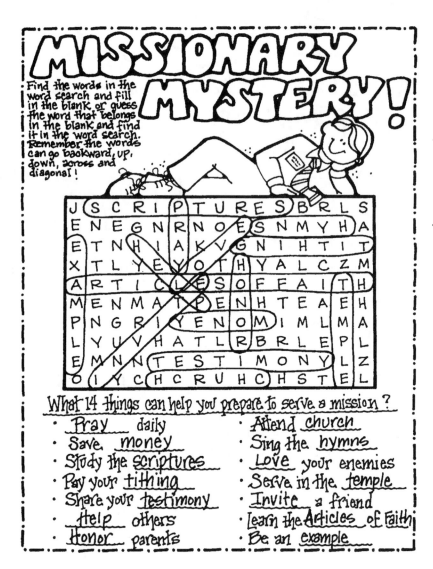

MISSIONARY MYSTERY!

Find the words in the word search and fill in the blank or guess the word that belongs in the blank and find it in the word search. Remember the words can go backward, up, down, across and diagonal!

What 14 things can help you prepare to serve a mission?

- <u>Pray</u> daily
- Save <u>money</u>
- Study the <u>scriptures</u>
- Pay your <u>tithing</u>
- Share your <u>testimony</u>
- <u>Help</u> others
- <u>Honor</u> parents
- Attend <u>church</u>
- Sing the <u>hymns</u>
- <u>Love</u> your enemies
- Serve in the <u>temple</u>
- <u>Invite</u> a friend
- Learn the <u>Articles of Faith</u>
- Be an <u>example</u>

YOU'LL NEED: *Copy of *Missionary Mystery! Word Search* (page 89) and Scripture Challenge Card 44 (page 115)for each child; pencils and markers.

Review Discussion: What steps have you taken and can take in the future to share the gospel? See page 156 in the *Primary 7 New Testament Manual.*

ACTIVITIES: · *Missionary Mystery! Word Search:* Help children learn ways they can prepare for a mission now and in the future with this Missionary Mystery! word search. Follow directions.

· *Scripture Challenge:* See details on page 93 (card on page 115).

ANSWERS:
- <u>Pray</u> daily
- Save <u>money</u>
- Study the <u>scriptures</u>
- Pay your <u>tithing</u>
- Share your <u>testimony</u>
- <u>Help</u> others
- <u>Honor</u> parents
- Attend <u>church</u>
- Sing the <u>hymns</u>
- <u>Love</u> your enemies
- Serve in the <u>temple</u>
- <u>Invite</u> a friend
- Learn the <u>Articles of Faith</u>
- Be an <u>example</u>

THOUGHT TREAT (when appropriate): Mission Munches Tracting Mix. Tell children, "Missionaries are always hungry when they go tracting (knocking on doors, telling others about the gospel). If you prepare now and learn to make your own Mission Munches, you won't have to go home for dinner when the Spirit tells you to knock on one more door."

To Make Tracting Mix:
1. Combine equal portions of these items and munch away!
2. Mix: Granola, nuts, sunflower seeds, dried fruit (pineapple, papaya, raisins, bananas, pears, and apples).

MISSIONARY MYSTERY!

Find the words in the word search and fill in the blank or guess the word that belongs in the blank and find it in the word search. Remember the words can go backward, up, down, across and diagonal!

```
J S C R I P T U R E S B R L S
E N E G N R N O E S N M Y H A
E T N H I A K V G N I H T I T
X T L Y E Y O T H Y A L C Z M
A R T I C L E S O F F A I T H
M E N M A T P E N H T E A E H
P N G R I Y E N O M I L M L A
L Y U V H A T L R B R L E P L
E M N N T E S T I M O N Y L Z
O I Y C H C R U H C H S T E L
```

What 14 things can help you prepare to serve a mission?

- _____ daily
- Save _____
- Study the _____
- Pay your _____
- Share your _____
- _____ others
- _____ parents
- Attend _____
- Sing the _____
- _____ your enemies
- Serve in the _____
- _____ a friend
- Learn the _____
- Be an _____

Lesson 45 — Spiritual Gifts: I Will Learn to Use My Spiritual Gifts

(Gifts of the Spirit Crossword Puzzle)

YOU'LL NEED: *Copy of *Gifts of the Spirit Crossword Puzzle* (page 91) and *Scripture Challenge Card 45* (page 116) for each child; pencils and markers.

ACTIVITIES: • *Gifts of the Spirit Crossword Puzzle:* This crossword puzzle will help children learn more about the gifts of the Spirit that they can receive from the Holy Ghost. Remind them that as they are righteous they can receive these gifts. If they are unrighteous, these gifts will be taken away. Imagine what it would be like without these gifts once you have enjoyed them. (1) *Color crossword. (2) Find the different gifts of the Spirit that are written across and down. Look up the scriptures to find the missing words. (3) After puzzle is complete, check your answers:
✔ *Across:* 3-revelation, 4-healed, 6-Holy Ghost, 7-healing, 8-tongues
✔ *Down:* 1-prophecy, 2-visions, 5-conversion

• *Scripture Challenge:* See details on page 93 (card on page 116).

Review Enrichment Activity 2 (page 160) in the *Primary 7 New Testament Manual.*

THOUGHT TREAT (when appropriate): Granola Bar Gift. Wrap a granola bar in gift wrap and tie with a ribbon. Tell children to open the gift bar and chew. As you chew, think of "chew"sing the right to be worthy to receive these sweet spiritual gifts from the Holy Ghost (review the completed puzzle).

Lesson 46 — Second Coming: I Will Be Ready When Jesus Comes Again

(Second Coming Checklist)

YOU'LL NEED: *Copy of *Second Coming Checklist* (page 92) and *Scripture Challenge Card 46* (page 116) for each child, pencils, and markers.

ACTIVITIES: • *Second Coming Checklist:* Help children think ahead to the day that the Savior will come. One day Jesus Christ will return to the earth, although no man knows when he will come. Ask children to ask themselves, *"If the Savior came to my house today, what would I do? What would I say?"* Would you want to hide some actions and start doing others? Use this Second Coming Checklist to see if you are ready for the Savior to come. Place a check mark in the square by things you would change to be ready for the Savior when he comes again. • *Scripture Challenge:* See details on page 93 (card on page 116).

Review Enrichment Activity 2 (page 165) in the *Primary 7 New Testament Manual.*

THOUGHT TREAT (when appropriate): Second Coming Smile Sandwiches. Spread cream cheese between two slices of bread. Cut off crust and cut sandwich into four parts. Make a smile face on top of each sandwich with a tube of processed cheese. Give each child one or two. Tell children that Jesus wants us to be happy. He wants us to be ready when He comes, by choosing the right each day.

GIFTS
OF THE SPIRIT

ACROSS

3. Luke 2:25-26
   D&C 46:22
4. Mark 5:25-34
   D&C 46:19
6. Gifts are given by...
   (Godhead member)
7. Acts 14:8-10
8. Acts 2:4-6

DOWN

1. Acts 2:14-18
2. 7th Article of Faith (4th gift)
5. Acts 9:1-20

SECOND COMING

CHECKLIST

If the Savior were to come to my house today, what would I do? What would I say? Check the actions you would change.

- [ ] Change the channel on the T.V. or turn it off?
- [ ] Change the music I am listening to?
- [ ] Pay an honest tithing?
- [ ] Read the scriptures more?
- [ ] Change the jokes I tell?

- [ ] Speak kinder words to others?
- [ ] Help my neighbors more?
- [ ] Go to bed early and rise early?
- [ ] Eat healthier foods?
- [ ] Wear more modest clothing?
- [ ] Pray more?

- [ ] Treat my friends differently?
- [ ] Visit the sick and lonely?
- [ ] Attend all my church meetings?
- [ ] Read different magazines or books?

Front and Back Cover for Scripture Challenge Cards #1-46
to Match Lessons #1-46 in Primary 7* New Testament Manual.

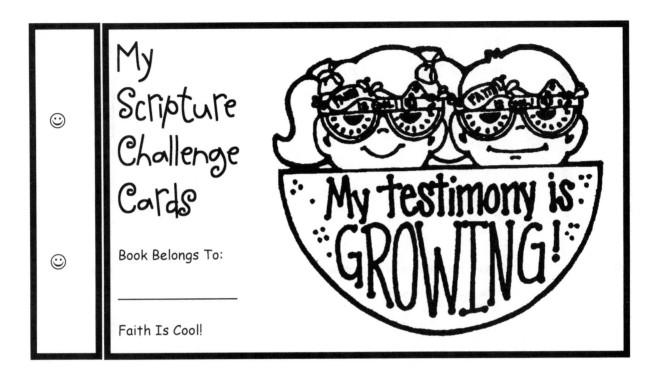

My
Scripture
Challenge
Cards

Book Belongs To:

_____

Faith Is Cool!

My testimony is GROWING!

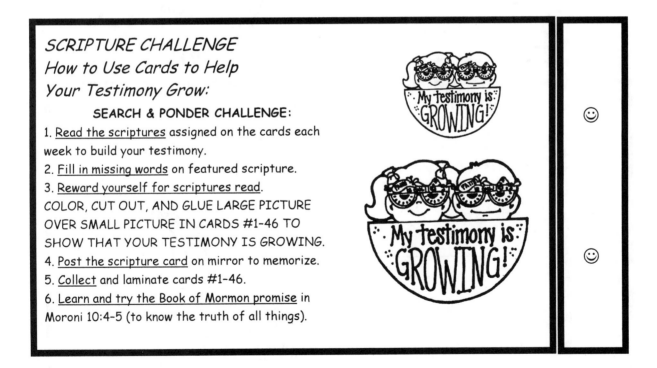

SCRIPTURE CHALLENGE
How to Use Cards to Help
Your Testimony Grow:

SEARCH & PONDER CHALLENGE:

1. Read the scriptures assigned on the cards each week to build your testimony.

2. Fill in missing words on featured scripture.

3. Reward yourself for scriptures read. COLOR, CUT OUT, AND GLUE LARGE PICTURE OVER SMALL PICTURE IN CARDS #1-46 TO SHOW THAT YOUR TESTIMONY IS GROWING.

4. Post the scripture card on mirror to memorize.

5. Collect and laminate cards #1-46.

6. Learn and try the Book of Mormon promise in Moroni 10:4-5 (to know the truth of all things).

Scriptures:
I Will Read the Scriptures to Learn of Jesus

1

> **SEARCH & PONDER CHALLENGE:**
> Read: 2 Timothy 3:14-17

2 Timothy 3:15 "From a child thou hast known the __ __ __ __ scriptures, which are able to make thee unto salvation through faith which is in Christ Jesus."

Matthew 22:29 "Jesus answered and said unto them, Ye do __ __ __ [wrong], not knowing the scriptures, nor the __ __ __ __ __ of God."

Jesus Christ:
Jesus Volunteered to Be Our Savior

2

> **SEARCH & PONDER CHALLENGE:**
> Read: Moses 4:1-4

Moses 4:3-4 "Wherefore, because that Satan __ __ __ __ __ __ __ __ __ against me, and sought to destroy the __ __ __ __ __ __ __ of man, which I the Lord God had given him, and also, that I should give unto him mine own power; by the power of mine Only Begotten, I caused that he should be cast down; And he became Satan, yea, even the devil, the father of all __ __ __ __, to deceive and to blind men, and to lead them captive."

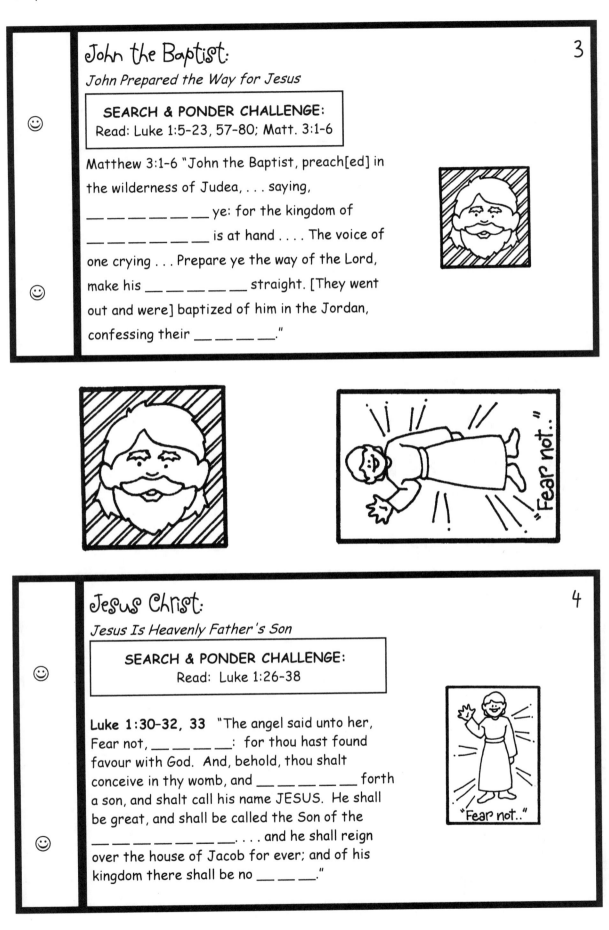

John the Baptist:

John Prepared the Way for Jesus

3

SEARCH & PONDER CHALLENGE:
Read: Luke 1:5-23, 57-80; Matt. 3:1-6

Matthew 3:1-6 "John the Baptist, preach[ed] in the wilderness of Judea, . . . saying, _ _ _ _ _ _ ye: for the kingdom of _ _ _ _ _ _ is at hand . . . . The voice of one crying . . . Prepare ye the way of the Lord, make his _ _ _ _ _ straight. [They went out and were] baptized of him in the Jordan, confessing their _ _ _ _ _."

Jesus Christ:

Jesus Is Heavenly Father's Son

4

SEARCH & PONDER CHALLENGE:
Read: Luke 1:26-38

Luke 1:30-32, 33 "The angel said unto her, Fear not, _ _ _ _: for thou hast found favour with God. And, behold, thou shalt conceive in thy womb, and _ _ _ _ _ forth a son, and shalt call his name JESUS. He shall be great, and shall be called the Son of the _ _ _ _ _ _ _ _ . . . . and he shall reign over the house of Jacob for ever; and of his kingdom there shall be no _ _ _."

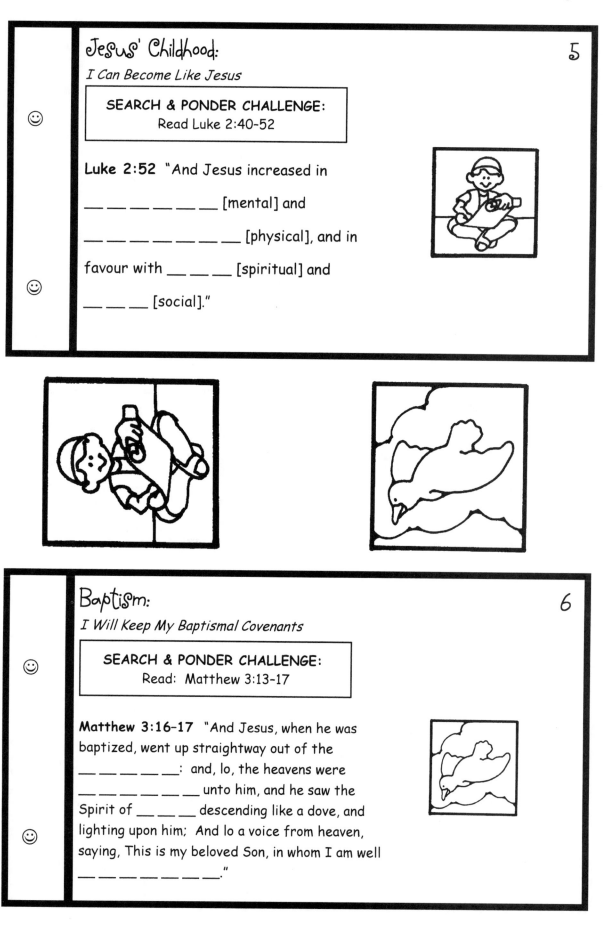

Jesus' Childhood:

I Can Become Like Jesus

SEARCH & PONDER CHALLENGE:
Read Luke 2:40-52

5

☺

☺

Luke 2:52 "And Jesus increased in

_ _ _ _ _ _ _ [mental] and

_ _ _ _ _ _ _ _ [physical], and in

favour with _ _ _ [spiritual] and

_ _ _ [social]."

Baptism:

I Will Keep My Baptismal Covenants

SEARCH & PONDER CHALLENGE:
Read: Matthew 3:13-17

6

☺

Matthew 3:16-17 "And Jesus, when he was
baptized, went up straightway out of the
_ _ _ _ _ _: and, lo, the heavens were
_ _ _ _ _ _ unto him, and he saw the
Spirit of _ _ _ descending like a dove, and
lighting upon him; And lo a voice from heaven,
saying, This is my beloved Son, in whom I am well
_ _ _ _ _ _ _."

☺

Temptation:

7

I Will Follow Jesus and Resist Temptation

SEARCH & PONDER CHALLENGE:
Read Matthew 4:1-11

☺

Matthew 4:3-4 "And when the

__ __ __ __ __ __ __ came to him, he said, If

thou be the Son of __ __ __, command that

these stones be made __ __ __ __ __. But he

☺ answered and said, It is written, Man shall not

live by bread alone, but by every __ __ __ __

that proceedeth out of the mouth of God."

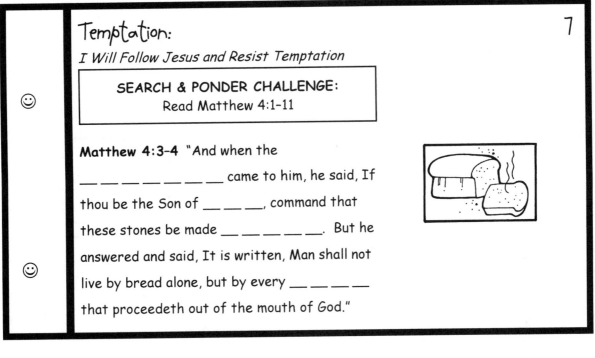

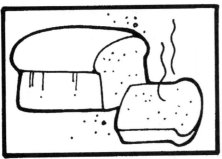

Respect:

8

I Will Show Heavenly Father and Jesus Respect

SEARCH & PONDER CHALLENGE:
Read: Matthew 21:12-14

☺

Matthew 21:12-14 "And Jesus went into the

temple of God, and __ __ __ __ out all of them

that sold and bought in the temple, and

overthrew the tables of the __ __ __ __ __-

changers, and the seats of them that sold doves,

And said unto them, It is written, My house shall

☺ be called the house of __ __ __ __ __ __; but

ye have made it a den of thieves."

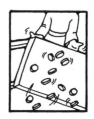

SCRIPTURE CHALLENGE CARDS for lessons 7 and 8

Apostles: 9

The Apostles Were Special Witnesses of Jesus

SEARCH & PONDER CHALLENGE:
Read Matthew 4:18-22

☺

☺

Matthew 4:18-29 "And Jesus, walking by the

___ ___ ___ of Galilee, saw two brethren, Simon

called ___ ___ ___ ___ ___, and Andrew his brother,

casting a net into the sea: for they were

fishers. And he saith unto them, Follow me, and

I will make you fishers of ___ ___ ___."

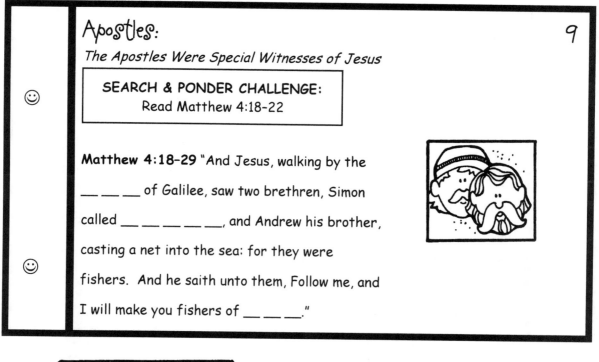

Sermon on the Mount: 10

Jesus Taught Us How to Return to Heaven

SEARCH & PONDER CHALLENGE:
Read: Matthew 5:3-11

☺

☺

Matthew 5:3 "Blessed are the poor in spirit
[who come unto ___ ___ (**3 Nephi 12:3**)], for
theirs is the kingdom of heaven."

Matthew 5:6 "Blessed are they which do hunger
and thirst after righteousness for they shall be
___ ___ ___ ___ ___ ___ [with the ___ ___ ___ ___
Ghost (**3 Nephi 12:6**)]."

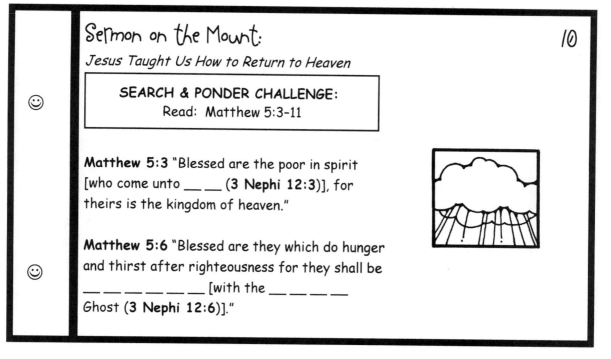

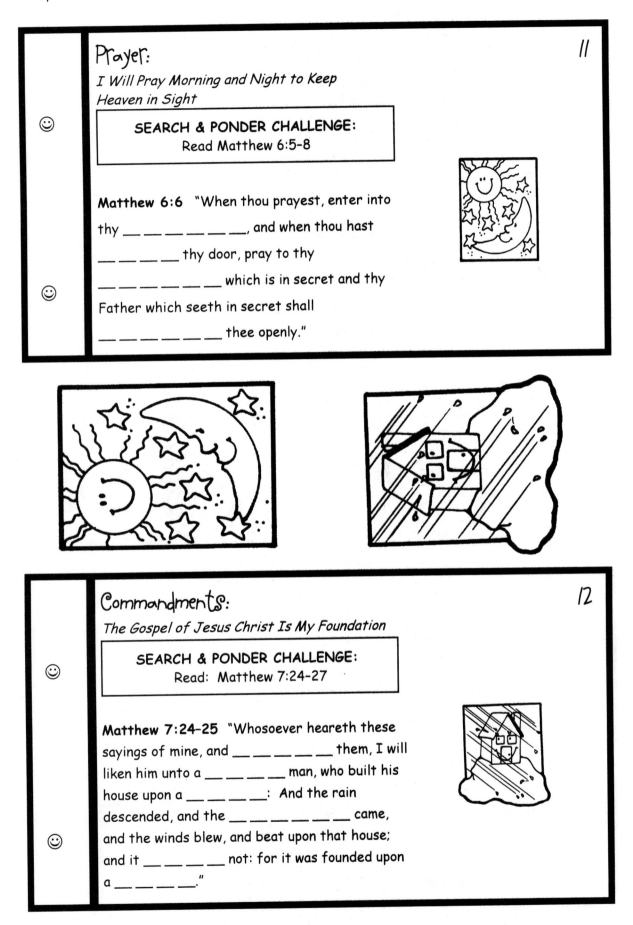

Prayer: 11

I Will Pray Morning and Night to Keep Heaven in Sight

SEARCH & PONDER CHALLENGE:
Read Matthew 6:5–8

Matthew 6:6 "When thou prayest, enter into thy _ _ _ _ _ _ _, and when thou hast _ _ _ _ _ thy door, pray to thy _ _ _ _ _ _ _ which is in secret and thy Father which seeth in secret shall _ _ _ _ _ _ _ thee openly."

Commandments: 12

The Gospel of Jesus Christ Is My Foundation

SEARCH & PONDER CHALLENGE:
Read: Matthew 7:24–27

Matthew 7:24–25 "Whosoever heareth these sayings of mine, and _ _ _ _ _ them, I will liken him unto a _ _ _ _ _ man, who built his house upon a _ _ _ _ _: And the rain descended, and the _ _ _ _ _ _ _ came, and the winds blew, and beat upon that house; and it _ _ _ _ _ not: for it was founded upon a _ _ _ _ _."

SCRIPTURE CHALLENGE CARDS for lessons 11 and 12

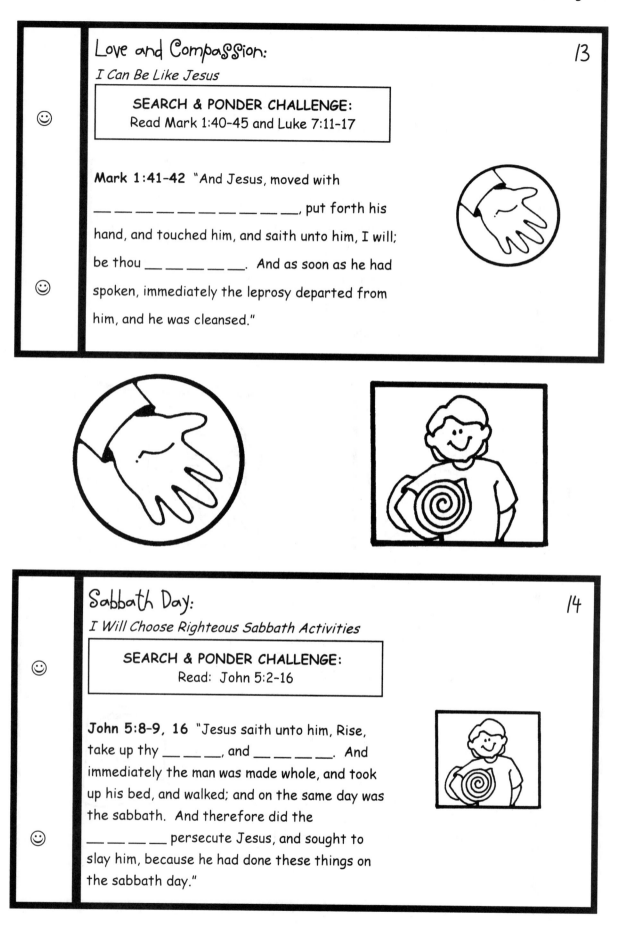

Love and Compassion: 13

I Can Be Like Jesus

SEARCH & PONDER CHALLENGE:
Read Mark 1:40-45 and Luke 7:11-17

Mark 1:41-42 "And Jesus, moved with

_ _ _ _ _ _ _ _ _ _ _, put forth his

hand, and touched him, and saith unto him, I will;

be thou _ _ _ _ _. And as soon as he had

spoken, immediately the leprosy departed from

him, and he was cleansed."

Sabbath Day: 14

I Will Choose Righteous Sabbath Activities

SEARCH & PONDER CHALLENGE:
Read: John 5:2-16

John 5:8-9, 16 "Jesus saith unto him, Rise,

take up thy _ _ _, and _ _ _ _. And

immediately the man was made whole, and took

up his bed, and walked; and on the same day was

the sabbath. And therefore did the

_ _ _ _ persecute Jesus, and sought to

slay him, because he had done these things on

the sabbath day."

Priesthood: 15

Heavenly Keys

| SEARCH & PONDER CHALLENGE: |
| Read Mark 4:35–41 |

☺

Mark 4:37–39 "And there arose a great
___ ___ ___ ___ ___ of wind, and the waves beat into
the ship, so that it was now ___ ___ ___ ___. . . .
[The disciples] awoke [Jesus], and [said] unto
him, Master, carest thou not that we perish?
And he arose, and rebuked the ___ ___ ___ ___, and
said unto the sea, Peace, be still. And the wind
ceased, and there was a great calm."

☺

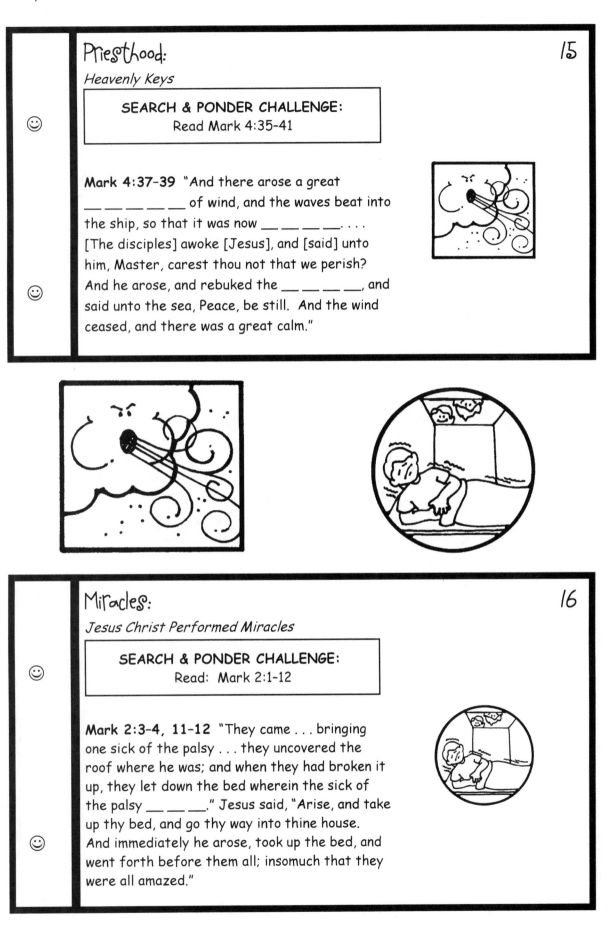

Miracles: 16

Jesus Christ Performed Miracles

| SEARCH & PONDER CHALLENGE: |
| Read: Mark 2:1–12 |

☺

Mark 2:3–4, 11–12 "They came . . . bringing
one sick of the palsy . . . they uncovered the
roof where he was; and when they had broken it
up, they let down the bed wherein the sick of
the palsy ___ ___ ___." Jesus said, "Arise, and take
up thy bed, and go thy way into thine house.
And immediately he arose, took up the bed, and
went forth before them all; insomuch that they
were all amazed."

☺

Parables:

17

I Will Live Like Jesus and Keep His Commandments

SEARCH & PONDER CHALLENGE:
Read Matthew 13:1-9

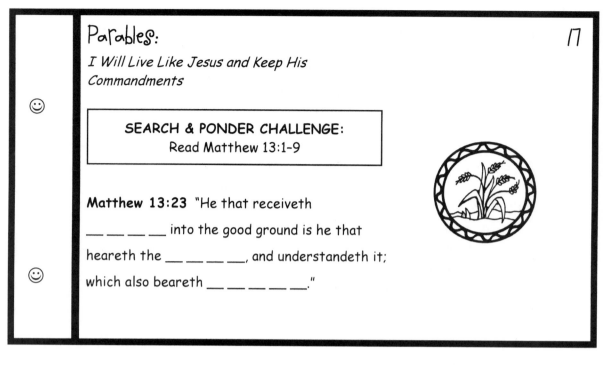

Matthew 13:23 "He that receiveth

__ __ __ __ into the good ground is he that

heareth the __ __ __ __, and understandeth it;

which also beareth __ __ __ __ __."

Faith:

18

I Can Overcome Trials With the Help of Jesus

SEARCH & PONDER CHALLENGE:
Read: John 9:1-38

John 9:10-11 "Said they unto him, How were

thine __ __ __ __ opened? He answered and

said, A man that is called Jesus made

__ __ __ __, and anointed mine eyes, and said

unto me, Go to the pool of Siloam, and

__ __ __ __: and I went and washed, and I

received sight."

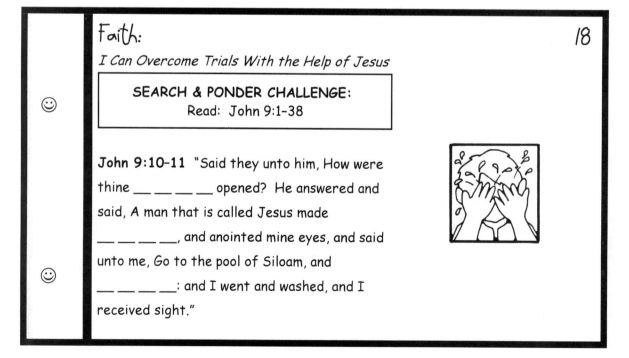

Fellowship: 19

I Will Help Those Who Are Less Active Return

SEARCH & PONDER CHALLENGE:
Read Luke 15:11-32

Luke 15:21-22, 24 "And the son said unto him, Father, I have __ __ __ __ __ __ __ against heaven, and in thy sight, and am no more worthy to be called thy son. But the father said to his servants, Bring forth the __ __ __ __ robe, and put it on him. . . . For this my son was dead, and is alive again."

Love Others: 20

I Will Show Love Like the Good Samaritan

SEARCH & PONDER CHALLENGE:
Read: Luke 10:25-37

Luke 10:25, 27 "A certain lawyer stood up, and tempted him [Jesus], saying, Master, what shall I do to __ __ __ __ __ __ __ __ eternal life? He answering said, Thou shalt __ __ __ __ the Lord thy God with all thy heart, and with all thy soul, and with all thy strength, and with all thy mind; and thy neighbour as __ __ __ __ __ __ __ __."

SCRIPTURE CHALLENGE CARDS for lessons 19 and 20

Gratitude: 21
Jesus Healed Ten Lepers and Only One Thanked Him

| SEARCH & PONDER CHALLENGE: |
| Read Luke 17:12-19 |

Luke 17:12–15 "And he [Jesus] . . . met ten men that were __ __ __ __ __ __, which stood afar off: And they lifted up their voices and said, Jesus, Master, have mercy on us. And . . . they were cleansed. And one of them, when he saw that he was healed, turned back, and with a loud __ __ __ __ __ glorified God."

Forgiveness: 22
I Will Be Merciful and Forgiving

| SEARCH & PONDER CHALLENGE: |
| Read: Matthew 18:21-35 |

Matthew 18:21–22 "Then came Peter to him, and said, Lord, how oft shall my brother __ __ __ against me, and I forgive him? till seven times? Jesus saith unto him, I say not unto thee, Until seven times: but, Until seventy times __ __ __ __ __."

Good Shepherd:

I Will Follow Jesus   23

SEARCH & PONDER CHALLENGE:
Read John 10:1-18

John 10:4, 16 "And when he putteth forth his own sheep, he goeth before them, and the sheep __ __ __ __ __ __ __ him: for they know his voice.... Other sheep I have, which are not of this fold: they also I must bring, and they shall __ __ __ __ my __ __ __ __ __ and there shall be one fold, and one shepherd."

Tithes and Offerings:

Windows of Heaven   24

SEARCH & PONDER CHALLENGE:
Read: Mark 12:41-44

Mark 12:41-44 "People cast money into the treasury: and many that were rich cast in much. And there came a certain __ __ __ __ widow, and she threw in two mites.... [Jesus said] This poor widow hath cast __ __ __ __ in, than all they which have cast into the treasury: For all they did cast in of their abundance; but she of her want did cast in __ __ __ that she had, even all her living."

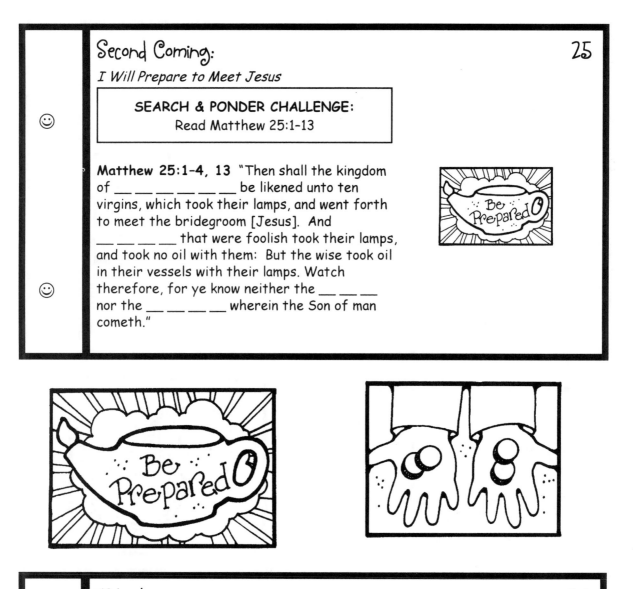

Second Coming: 25

I Will Prepare to Meet Jesus

> **SEARCH & PONDER CHALLENGE:**
> Read Matthew 25:1-13

Matthew 25:1-4, 13 "Then shall the kingdom of __ __ __ __ __ __ be likened unto ten virgins, which took their lamps, and went forth to meet the bridegroom [Jesus]. And __ __ __ __ that were foolish took their lamps, and took no oil with them: But the wise took oil in their vessels with their lamps. Watch therefore, for ye know neither the __ __ __ nor the __ __ __ __ wherein the Son of man cometh."

Talents: 26

I Will Use My Talents to Serve Others

> **SEARCH & PONDER CHALLENGE:**
> Read: Matthew 25:14-30

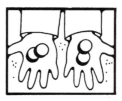

Matthew 25:22-23 "He also that had received two talents came and said, Lord, thou deliveredst unto me two talents: behold, I have __ __ __ __ __ __ two other talents beside them. His lord said unto him, Well done, good and faithful servant; thou hast been faithful over a few things, I will make thee __ __ __ __ __ over many things: enter thou into the __ __ __ of the lord."

Service: 27

Parable of the Sheep and Goats

SEARCH & PONDER CHALLENGE:
Read Matthew 25:35-40

Matthew 25:37-38, 40 "When saw we thee an hungred, and __ __ __ thee? or thirsty, and gave thee __ __ __ __ __? When saw we thee a stranger and took thee __ __? or naked, and __ __ __ __ __ __ __ __ thee? And the King shall answer and say unto them, Verily I say unto you, Inasmuch as ye have __ __ __ __ it unto one of the least of these my brethren, ye have done it unto __ __."

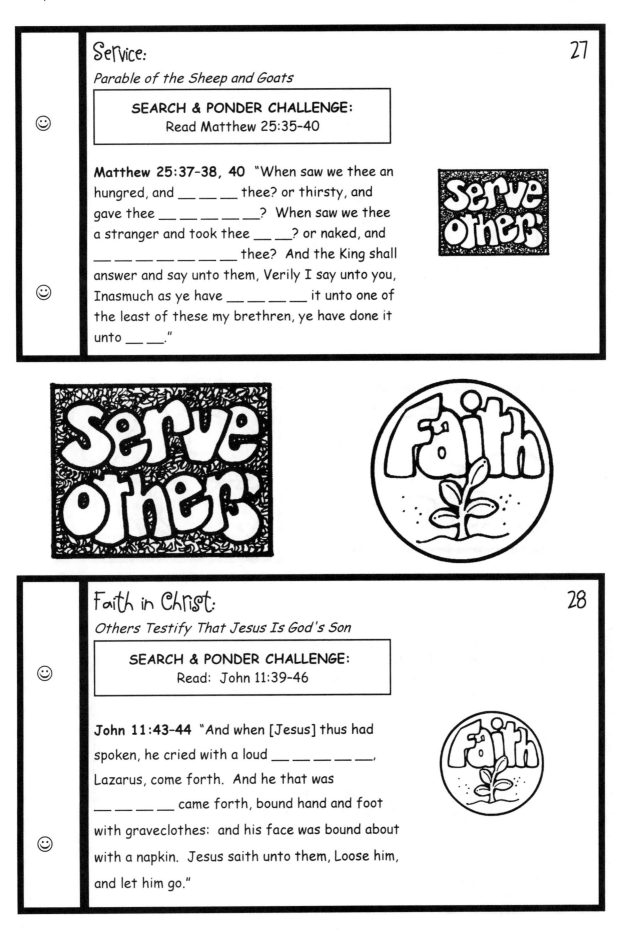

Faith in Christ: 28

Others Testify That Jesus Is God's Son

SEARCH & PONDER CHALLENGE:
Read: John 11:39-46

John 11:43-44 "And when [Jesus] thus had spoken, he cried with a loud __ __ __ __ __ __, Lazarus, come forth. And he that was __ __ __ __ __ came forth, bound hand and foot with graveclothes: and his face was bound about with a napkin. Jesus saith unto them, Loose him, and let him go."

SCRIPTURE CHALLENGE CARDS for lessons 27 and 28

Sacrament: 29

I Will Think of Jesus

SEARCH & PONDER CHALLENGE:
Read Mark 14:12-26

Mark 14:22-24 "And as they did eat, Jesus took bread, and blessed, and brake it, and gave to them, and said, Take eat: this is my __ __ __ __. And he took the cup, and when he had given thanks, he gave it to them: and they all drank of it. And he said unto them, This is my __ __ __ __ __ of the new testament, which is shed for many."

Repentance: 30

Jesus Helped Me Overcome Sin and Death

SEARCH & PONDER CHALLENGE:
Read: Matthew 26:36-46

Matthew 26:41-43 "Watch and __ __ __ __, that ye enter not into temptation: the spirit indeed is willing, but the __ __ __ __ __ is weak. He went away again the second time, and prayed, saying, O my Father, if this cup may not pass away from me, except I drink it, thy will be done. And he came and found [the disciples] __ __ __ __ __ __ again."

Atonement: 31

Jesus Is Our Life Savior

| SEARCH & PONDER CHALLENGE: |
| Read Matthew 26:47-54 |

Matthew 26:53-54 "Thinkest thou that I cannot now __ __ __ __ to my Father, and he shall presently give me more than twelve legions of angels? But how then shall the scriptures be __ __ __ __ __ __ __ __ __, that thus it must be?"

Atonement: 32

Jesus Suffered for Me

| SEARCH & PONDER CHALLENGE: |
| Read: Matthew 27:34-50 |

Luke 23:33-34 "When they were come to . . . Calvary, there they crucified him . . . Then said Jesus, Father, forgive them; for they know not what they __ __." **Matthew 27:46, 50** "And about the ninth hour Jesus cried with a loud voice, saying . . . My God, my God, why hast thou forsaken me? Jesus, when he had cried again . . . yielded up the __ __ __ __ __ [his spirit left his body]."

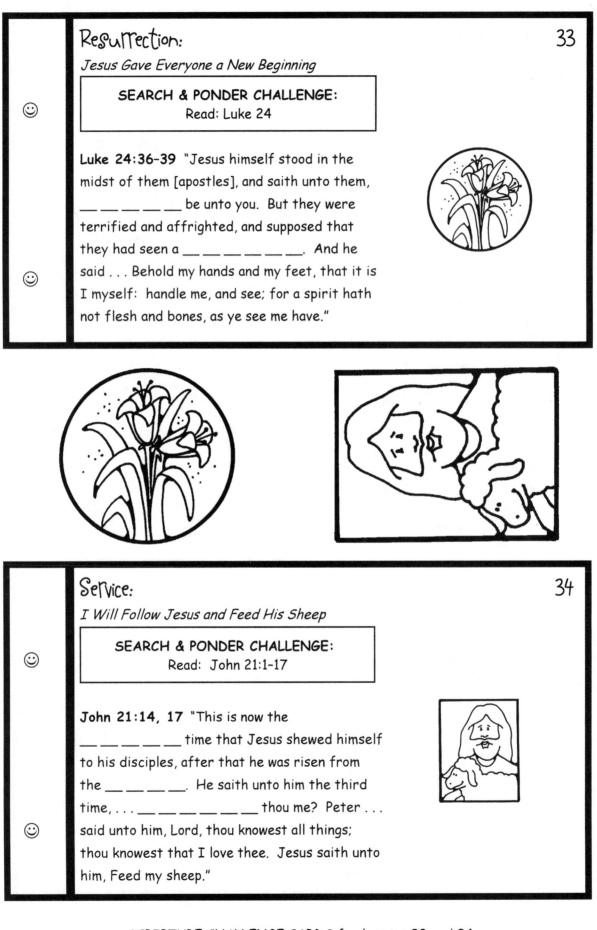

Resurrection: 33

Jesus Gave Everyone a New Beginning

> **SEARCH & PONDER CHALLENGE:**
> Read: Luke 24

Luke 24:36–39 "Jesus himself stood in the midst of them [apostles], and saith unto them, __ __ __ __ __ __ be unto you. But they were terrified and affrighted, and supposed that they had seen a __ __ __ __ __ __. And he said . . . Behold my hands and my feet, that it is I myself: handle me, and see; for a spirit hath not flesh and bones, as ye see me have."

Service: 34

I Will Follow Jesus and Feed His Sheep

> **SEARCH & PONDER CHALLENGE:**
> Read: John 21:1–17

John 21:14, 17 "This is now the __ __ __ __ __ time that Jesus shewed himself to his disciples, after that he was risen from the __ __ __ __. He saith unto him the third time, . . . __ __ __ __ __ __ __ __ thou me? Peter . . . said unto him, Lord, thou knowest all things; thou knowest that I love thee. Jesus saith unto him, Feed my sheep."

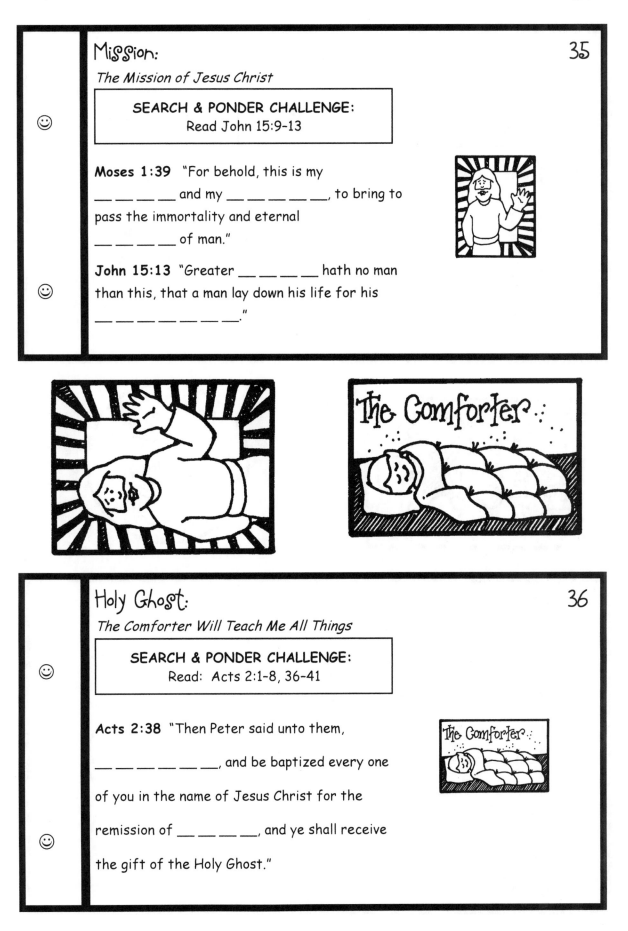

Mission: 35

The Mission of Jesus Christ

> **SEARCH & PONDER CHALLENGE:**
> Read John 15:9–13

Moses 1:39 "For behold, this is my
__ __ __ __ and my __ __ __ __ __, to bring to
pass the immortality and eternal
__ __ __ __ of man."

John 15:13 "Greater __ __ __ __ hath no man
than this, that a man lay down his life for his
__ __ __ __ __ __ __."

The Comforter

Holy Ghost: 36

The Comforter Will Teach Me All Things

> **SEARCH & PONDER CHALLENGE:**
> Read: Acts 2:1–8, 36–41

Acts 2:38 "Then Peter said unto them,
__ __ __ __ __ __, and be baptized every one
of you in the name of Jesus Christ for the
remission of __ __ __ __, and ye shall receive
the gift of the Holy Ghost."

The Comforter

Testimony: 37

I Can Bear My Testimony

> **SEARCH & PONDER CHALLENGE:**
> Read Matthew 16:13-17 and Acts 5:29-32

Acts 4:31 "And when they had prayed, the place was shaken where they were assembled together; and they were all __ __ __ __ __ __ with the Holy Ghost, and they __ __ __ __ __ the word of God with boldness."

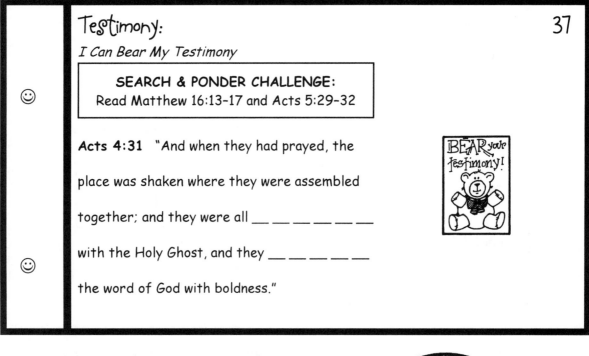

Honesty: 38

I Will Be Honest in Thought, Word, and Deed

> **SEARCH & PONDER CHALLENGE:**
> Read: Acts 4:32-5:10

Acts 4:32 "And the multitude of them that believed were of one __ __ __ __ __ and of one __ __ __ __: neither said any of them that ought of the things which he possessed was his own; but they had all things in __ __ __ __ __ __."

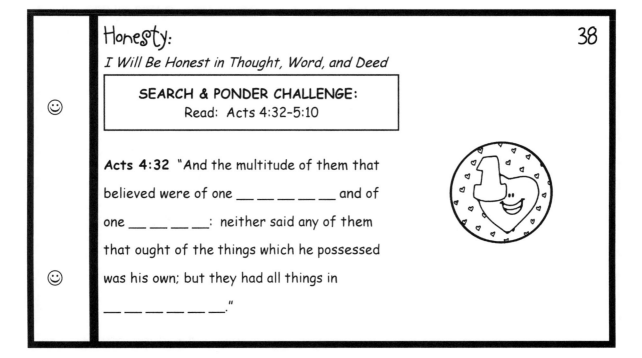

Godhead: 39

I Love Heavenly Father, Jesus Christ, and the Holy Ghost

> **SEARCH & PONDER CHALLENGE:**
> Read Acts 7:54-60 and D&C 130:22-23

☺

Acts 7:55 "He being full of the __ __ __ __ - __ __ __ __ __, looked up stedfastly into heaven, and saw the glory of God, and Jesus standing on the right hand of God."

D&C 130:22 "The Father has a __ __ __ __ of flesh and bones . . . the Son also; but the Holy Ghost has not a body of __ __ __ __ __ and bones, but is a personage of Spirit."

☺

Missionary: 40

Heavenly Father Wants Everyone to Learn the Gospel

> **SEARCH & PONDER CHALLENGE:**
> Read: Acts 10:36-43 and 11:15-18

☺

Acts 10:42-43 "And he commanded us to __ __ __ __ __ __ unto the people, and to testify that it is he which was ordained of God to be the Judge of quick and dead. To him give all the prophets witness, that through his name whosoever believeth in him shall receive remission of __ __ __ __."

☺

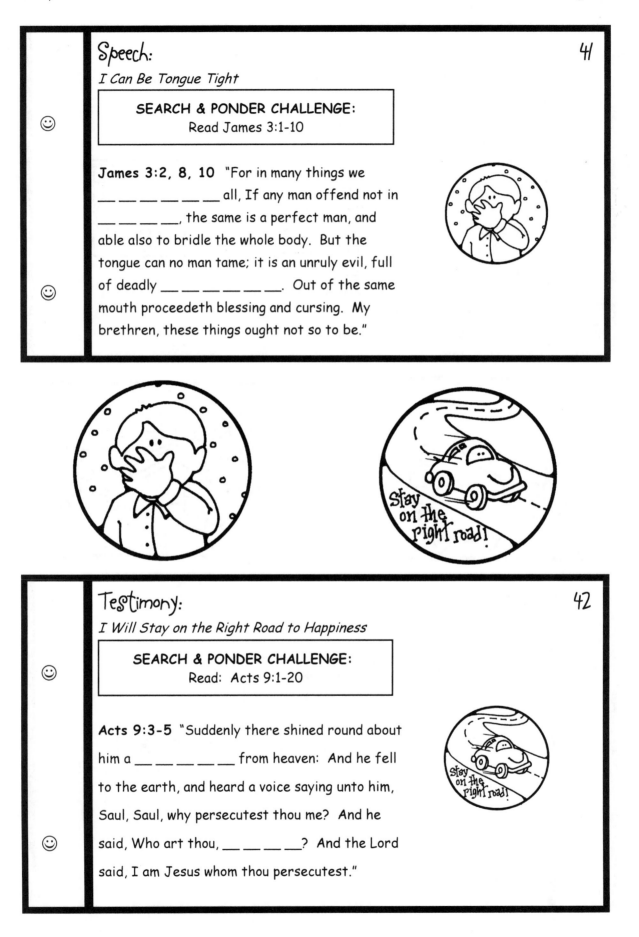

Speech: 41

I Can Be Tongue Tight

SEARCH & PONDER CHALLENGE:
Read James 3:1-10

James 3:2, 8, 10 "For in many things we
__ __ __ __ __ __ __ all, If any man offend not in
__ __ __ __ __, the same is a perfect man, and
able also to bridle the whole body. But the
tongue can no man tame; it is an unruly evil, full
of deadly __ __ __ __ __ __ __. Out of the same
mouth proceedeth blessing and cursing. My
brethren, these things ought not so to be."

Testimony: 42

I Will Stay on the Right Road to Happiness

SEARCH & PONDER CHALLENGE:
Read: Acts 9:1-20

Acts 9:3-5 "Suddenly there shined round about
him a __ __ __ __ __ __ from heaven: And he fell
to the earth, and heard a voice saying unto him,
Saul, Saul, why persecutest thou me? And he
said, Who art thou, __ __ __ __ __? And the Lord
said, I am Jesus whom thou persecutest."

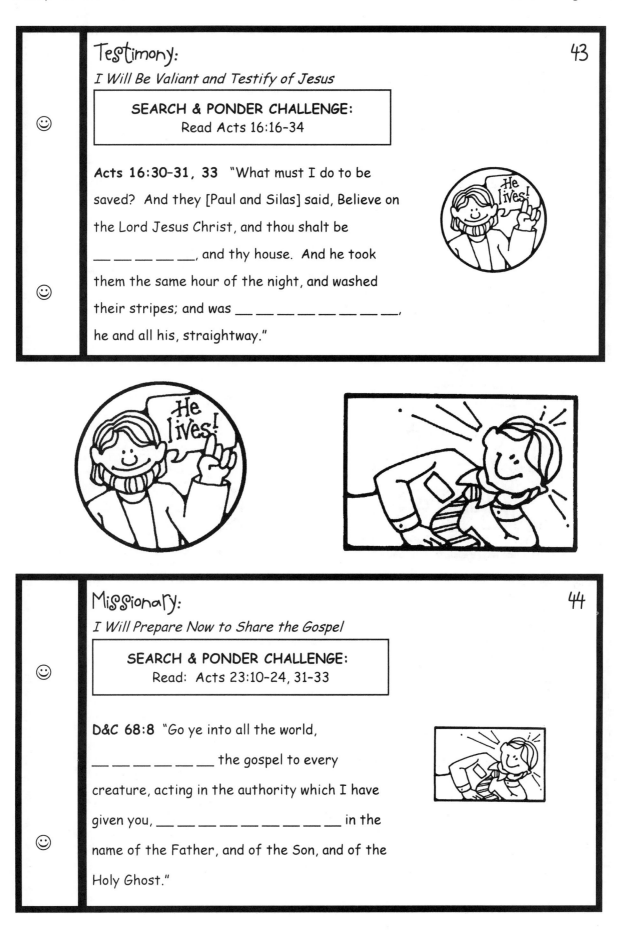

Testimony: 43

I Will Be Valiant and Testify of Jesus

SEARCH & PONDER CHALLENGE:
Read Acts 16:16-34

Acts 16:30-31, 33 "What must I do to be saved? And they [Paul and Silas] said, Believe on the Lord Jesus Christ, and thou shalt be ___ ___ ___ ___ ___, and thy house. And he took them the same hour of the night, and washed their stripes; and was ___ ___ ___ ___ ___ ___ ___ ___, he and all his, straightway."

Missionary: 44

I Will Prepare Now to Share the Gospel

SEARCH & PONDER CHALLENGE:
Read: Acts 23:10-24, 31-33

D&C 68:8 "Go ye into all the world, ___ ___ ___ ___ ___ ___ the gospel to every creature, acting in the authority which I have given you, ___ ___ ___ ___ ___ ___ ___ ___ in the name of the Father, and of the Son, and of the Holy Ghost."

Spiritual Gifts: 45

I Will Learn to Use My Spiritual Gifts

SEARCH & PONDER CHALLENGE:
Read Acts 28:111

Acts 28:89 "The father of Publius lay sick of a fever . . . to whom Paul entered in, and __ __ __ __ __ __, and laid his hands on him, and __ __ __ __ __ __ him. So when this was done, others also, which had __ __ __ __ __ __ __ __ in the island, came, and were healed."

Gifts of the Spirit

Gifts of the Spirit

Will you be ready?

Second Coming: 46

I Will Be Ready When Jesus Comes Again

SEARCH & PONDER CHALLENGE:
Pearl of Great Price
Joseph Smith—Matthew 1:4655

Pearl of Great Price Joseph Smith—Matthew 1:4648 "Watch, therefore, for you know not at what __ __ __ __ your Lord doth come . . . . If the good man . . . had known in what watch the thief would come, he would have watched, and would not have suffered his house to have been broken up, but would have been __ __ __ __ __. . . . Be ye also ready, for in such an hour as ye think not, [Jesus] the Son of Man cometh."

Will you be ready?